D1493293

THE FITZROY EDITION

COUNTRYMAN ON THE BROADS

THE FITZROY EDITION

OLIVER G. READY

Countryman on the Broads

EDITED BY
JOHN GERARD O'LEARY

INTRODUCTION BY
IAN NIALL

MACGIBBON & KEE

FIRST PUBLISHED 1910 UNDER THE TITLE OF
LIFE AND SPORT ON THE NORFOLK BROADS
THIS EDITION PUBLISHED 1967 BY MACGIBBON & KEE LTD
COPYRIGHT © MACGIBBON & KEE LTD 1967
PRINTED IN GREAT BRITAIN BY
COX & WYMAN LTD
LONDON, READING AND FAKENHAM

CONTENTS

FOREWORD

OLIVER GEORGE READY was born on the 18th of December 1864, the seventh son of Henry Ready, Rector of Waxham cum Palling, Norfolk: he was educated at Holt Grammar School and at Jesus College, Cambridge, where he graduated Bachelor of Arts in 1886. After leaving Cambridge, he became a school master for a while and then joined the Chinese Imperial Maritime Customs as a Commissioner; he used his experiences in China to write a book on Chinese customs. He died on the 31st of January 1940

In 1910 he published *Life and Sport on the Norfolk Broads*, which was inspired by his boyhood and youth on Hickling Broad. This volume is a selection from that work.

INTRODUCTION

No countryman lives in his ideal age, I think. In every generation the 'good old days' are invariably days in which a man's grandfather lived. At times, so far as I am concerned, some of the special magic derives from scenes depicted in the engravings of Bewick and the world of Colonel Hawker, and certainly the writing of Gilbert White and Richard Jefferies. There is a particular enchantment in accounts of a countryside we never knew, the green and golden worlds of mowers in meadows and great wagons on the endless stubbles and everything properly remote from the grime and squalor of cities. Oliver G. Ready wrote of his boyhood life in a book entitled *Life and Sport on the Norfolk Broads* with a touch of proper nostalgia, but only a touch. He balanced his account by revealing a rich store of accumulated knowledge that made his book regionally important in the way that Osgood MacKenzie's *A Hundred Years in the Highlands* was significant. It had an atmosphere, a time-set character that Messrs MacGibbon and Kee surely recognised when they considered reissuing the work.

Countryman on the Broads is a more appropriate title, perhaps, because the lore of the Broads, the peculiar ways of Norfolk, are faithfully recorded. One knows that a coot shoot with muzzle-loading guns is something that will never be again—Mr Ready armed himself with four guns—but even if gunners and guns could be found, even if that black mass of coots could be flushed from the reeds once again, we shall never know the characters who peopled the Broads and drove the fowl when Mr Ready was a boy. The ringing of pigs' noses with flattened nails is surely rarely done these days, but who would put a monkey in a pen to live with pigs and trust that all would go well, as it did, with the monkey becoming protector of the pigs and exerting greater influence over them as a result? The monkey's tail withered three inches a year, Mr Ready noted. He watched such things with a discerning eye, discovered that barley straw for bedding resulted in ferrets having ticks, and solved the mystery of how a coot's nest stays above the flood, being lightly woven about the stalks of reeds that moor it and let it rise and fall without becoming water-logged. Eating a custard of eggs of hedgesparrow, yellow hammer and chaffinch may have had no more serious result than a revulsion at the bitter taste, but once in the ruins of Waxham Abbey his life hung in the balance while he robbed a pigeon of its fledgings, dangling on a slender cord. Every man growing old may tell of like adventure as a boy, but not many of us can recreate our world and convey authentic atmosphere so thoroughly. Oliver Ready gave us his private world, the rectory where smugglers left a keg of brandy on the doorstep to warn the rector that his barn was being used to store contraband, and much else besides. He told of wherries and sailing races, the conversion of his punt to sail, at great cost in pets which he was compelled to sell to raise two pounds, described the trapping of sparrows to make sparrow pie, and the days when he went rabbitting and coursing hares, and brought it all, with charm and warmth, to a conclusion which I, for one, would echo— 'Present times may be more prosperous, new manners be more fine . . . still give *me* the old.'

Ian Niall

CHAPTER I

Waxham cum Palling

OUR neighbours in Waxham cum Palling were mostly farmers and labouring folk, with whom we were on the best of terms, and though in after years my lot has been thrown with many in higher spheres of life, I still like those old friends best, and am ever looking forward to the time when I shall be able to lay work aside and go back to live and die in my native place.

This neighbourhood on the east coast, alive with game, wildfowl, and countless varieties of beautiful birds both indigenous and migratory, was formerly the delta or estuary of a network of small rivers falling into the North Sea at different points. Partly, however, owing to natural causes, and partly owing to extensive drainage, many of these small rivers have long since ceased to exist, while large tracts of lagoon and marshland have been reclaimed.

Thirty years ago this land of sea-coast, fogs, gales, wrecks, marshes, rivers, lakes, boats and windmills, having no railway and only very bad roads, was still practically isolated, so that its inhabitants, living under peculiar conditions and largely thrown on their own resources, had developed types of character and speech very dissimilar to what prevailed elsewhere.

It was amongst and as one of these people, many of whom were unable to read or write, that I passed my boyhood, and as the strong and amusing types peculiar to this then almost foreign country have now all but vanished before the railroad, the board school, the bicycle and the motor-car, it may be that these reminiscences will prove of interest to others besides myself.

The narrow lane was so deeply pitted with ruts that it had all the appearance of a choppy sea, while towering up some eight or nine feet from broad water ditches on either side were dense tangles of bulrushes, flowering black-thorn, willows and feathery-plumed reeds, from out the shadowy depths of which reed-warblers and hay-jacks sent up a continuous chant of sweet, contented chattering. The sky was without a cloud, and the frequent cry of 'hold-jer' from busy haymakers sounded pleasantly on the morning air. It was one of those days in the life of a child which memory will treasure and hold undimmed for aye. The warm sun, the gentle breeze, the distant murmur of the sea, the perfect contentment – it is all as real to me now as then.

I may have been four years old or even five, as I trudged along in the wake of my four brothers, Harold, Matthew, Clement and Bob, all spick-and-span in home-made Scotch caps, Norfolk jackets of blue serge, and white duck trousers, *en route* to the Broad, and whose backward glances of irritation at being saddled with the care of such a brat in no wise marred my enjoyment. They *had* to take care of me, and I quite realized their sub-servient position.

As we turned a corner, the dear old Broad, gleaming like a sheet of silver in a grass-green frame, burst into view, its surface alive with glittering ripples dancing for very joy in the brilliant sunshine.

The little tarred, flat-bottomed boat was filled with clean, sweet-smelling marsh hay, most comfortable to sit or lie on, there being no seats. In two minutes we had embarked, and were being sedately quanted up the dyke towards the open Broad by Geoffrey. Before, however, we had gone a hundred yards the sedateness wore away, Clem and Bob simultaneously finding a broken oar under the hay and struggling for possession of it, so that to restore order Geoffrey splashed water at them with the quant, but, making a bad shot, sent it all over Harold, who, always very natty in his attire, was much irritated, and commenced to expostulate with considerable heat, moving a hand up and down chopperwise in order to emphasize his remarks. Mat took possession of the broken oar, leaving Clem and Bob still quarrelling, and vigorously helped to get the boat along, making it sheer about and roll in most exciting fashion: so that splashing, quarrelling, and rolling we made for the Second War Bush, a dense bed of reeds some half a mile distant. Being too young for navigation work, I gave my attention to the bullaces.

Just before reaching our destination, and when the uproar was at its highest, some one suddenly exclaimed: 'Old Tom!'

In a moment the broken oar was hidden under the hay, and we were all as quiet and frightened as mice, for coming straight towards us was the little punt, slowly sculled by Old Tom, with Grandson Albert sitting scared and huddled up on the after-part, steering with a quant. One could have heard a pin drop in our boat, and only Geoffrey stirred, quanting in most careful manner. There was no more 'Old Tom', but a most respectful 'Good morning, Mr Rudd', from us all as his boat passed, to which salutations, however, Mr Rudd vouchsafed no reply, although his strong, unshaven face, surmounted by an old seal-skin cap pulled down on one side, was turned towards us until we squirmed beneath the watching eye. As the boats gradually drew apart, we began to breathe again, though our conversation was carried on in whispers for a good ten minutes.

If only Old Tom had known how we feared, respected, and looked up to him, the golden heart in his rough old body must have warmed towards us. Perhaps he did know; nay, I think he must, or he never would have tolerated us as he did. Barely able to read or write, he was as thorough in his bad qualities as in his good, but, taking all in all, he had the most powerful personality, the kindest heart concealed by the gruffest manner, and the shrewdest head of any man I have ever met in his rank in life. In our eyes he was invincible and could do no wrong, while a word against him by outsiders we should have resented as a direct insult to ourselves.

A visit to the derelict was decided on. She was simply an old tarred hulk, masts and rigging having been removed. Her gross tonnage may have been sixty, but as I scrambled on all fours up the sloping deck she appeared to me a veritable leviathan. Green sword-rushes clustered thickly round as though to screen old age from prying eyes, while a hot sun pouring down caused the tar on her decks to soften and melt into little cracks and runnels. The hatches having been removed, her dark hold could be seen full of water, where floated numerous dead fish, such, doubtless, having swam in through some hole only to be poisoned by the tar.

Suddenly Bob lost his hold on the upper bulwark to which he had been clinging, and involuntarily slid across

the steeply-canting deck, but the softened tar stuck to his
white duck trousers, so that he travelled gently, and was
able to pull up at the lower bulwark instead of being shot
over it into the water. The idea at once caught hold, and
for the next half-hour or so we were all tobogganing hard,
turning round every few minutes for public inspection as
to whose garments had collected the most tar! Finally
Clem, who always seemed the unlucky one, accidentally
slid into the hold amongst the dead fish, thereby awakening a most awful stench, and when hauled out dripping,
vehemently declared he had been intentionally pushed in
by the others.

Wet, muddy, and tarred, we were home for one o'clock
dinner, delicious Norfolk dumplings and beef gravy,
followed by broad beans and bacon, being set before us,
upon which we fell like a swarm of locusts; and as the
cooked beans exactly resembled the little pink ears of our
monkey 'Ginney', I said so, for which remark I was
called 'a disgusting little wretch' by one of my sisters,
who furthermore complained that she could eat no more
as I had quite spoiled her appetite; over which misfortune
we boys did not grieve.

To get us out of the way, we thought, my brothers and
I were often packed off to the church of a neighbouring
clergyman, which was not more than a mile distant.

It was a grand old pile, built of flint stones from the
sea-shore, with leaden roof and massive square tower
wherein hung a peal of enormous bells, while the interior
showed a beautiful carved screen, noble oaken roofing,
and a high gallery at the west end, from where the choir
of respectable, elderly men and a few hobbledehoys
howled down doxologies, glory-bes and old-time hymns

of unvarying tune, to the accompaniment of concertinas, fiddles and clarionettes.

In the very centre of the church was a towering edifice commencing with the parish clerk's desk, above which was the clergyman's reading desk, above which, reached by way of a winding stair, was the pulpit, and above which again was an enormous sounding-board. The pews were of the loose-box type, having door and sides about four and a half feet high, so that when sitting down one was perfectly screened from view. Each pew was privately owned, and so could be fitted up and made comfortable with cushions, carpets and hassocks according to taste.

There was a grandeur, a venerableness, an atmosphere of restfulness and peace about the ancient edifice which raised it above all ordinary buildings and proclaimed God's House. An era of church restoration, however, was abroad, and the parish elders declared that the beautiful old temple must be 'restored'. The magnificent lead roof was stripped off, sold, and replaced by slates; the screen was torn down and cast out; the old three-decker pulpit was expelled; the comfortable and seclusive pews were supplanted by rows of varnished seats; the old stone pavement was replaced by bright and slippery tiles; the gallery was demolished; the frescoed walls scraped and plastered; in fact, the noble edifice, sanctified by centuries of worship, by generations of marriages, baptisms and burials, was destroyed, giving place to a modern building with pretty windows, gaudy floor, and rows of brightly-varnished seats: of a truth, it was 'swept and garnished'.

Our pew was a large, plain structure, though my brothers had done their best in the matter of decoration, its sides being thickly covered with pictures of ships, horses, dogs, etc., all laboriously carved with pocket-knives during long-winded sermons.

The adjoining pew belonged to an old woman named Judy Hatten, who was something of a local celebrity, owing to the fact of having long since lost every one of her teeth, besides being addicted to smoking a short clay pipe, and which, as she could get no grip on the stem with her bare gums, always hung bowl downwards when in action. Judy was also held to be something of a 'wise' woman, her dictum on the Sunday's preaching being especially sought after both on account of its conclusiveness as well as of its originality; for example, on a sermon preached from the text, 'There shall be weeping and gnashing of teeth', her mumbled verdict was 'What I say is, let them nayshe 'em as hev 'em'.

Judy had quite gratuitously set herself the task of looking after our behaviour during service, and whenever marbles accidentally fell on the resounding floor, or a quiet scuffle was taking place, her old poke-bonnet and wrinkled face would appear above the side of the pew, while a hoarse whisper parroted: 'Yow mussent maäke so much nise tegither.'

We naturally did not like our privacy being thus broken in upon, but were quite powerless to prevent it until a happy accident caused her to desist.

In order to carry out a difficult piece of carving, Harold one Sunday brought a gimlet in his pocket, and was just setting to work when some one suggested that if he bored a hole through the partition we could see old Judy at her devotions. The idea finding favour, Harold went at it with such a will that almost before we realized what he was doing, the gimlet shot through the thin boarding with a rush, Harold's knuckles fetching up on the partition with a thump which resounded all through the church, and was immediately followed by a piercing screech of pain and terror. The gimlet had penetrated poor old Judy's back and got wound up in her shawl! To jerk it out, bringing with it some pieces of wool, was the work of an instant. The parson stopped and looked round, there was a general movement as of people rising, while the sexton first came and glared at us sitting as quiet as mice, and then asked old Judy in a loud whisper what was the matter, to which the good old soul replied, 'It wor nor but the rheumatiz' that made her sing out; though what she said to us when people were 'going out' and no one else could hear, need not be repeated.

This 'neighbouring clergyman', who was also the squire, and known far and near as simply 'The Rarverand', was one of the now extinct sporting parsons, who, after spending the week in generous living, would preach to full congregations on Sunday. A man of kingly presence and mellow, stentorian voice, of most magnetic and dominating personality, a born swell, he was forgiven everything and literally worshipped by everyone who came in contact with him. Shooting, sailing, fishing, and coursing were his favourite amusements. Of greyhounds he kept about a dozen, and as the kennels were close to the church, the dogs would hear the well-known voice booming sonorously through the service, and set up in sympathy an answering chorus of yapping and baying, when the preacher would wheel majestically round and glare at his factotum, who, a little, bandy-legged, rotund person living solely in the reflected glory of his master and called by him 'Activity', would steal down the aisle on tiptoe, but with increasing pace, till he went out of the church door at a run, struggling, meanwhile, to get the dog whip out of the tail pocket of his tweed coat. In another minute a sudden silence, followed by yelps and howls of pain, would tell of his arrival at the kennels; and then, having restored order, he would very slowly return up the aisle, quivering at every step with the dignity of Justice invincible.

This occurrence took place twice every Sunday, being quite a recognized part of each service, and its omission would have given rise to general comment.

Next after the Broad, Palling beach took rank in our esteem as a happy hunting-ground, and a day on the firm, white sands, bathing and shrimping in the shallow lows when the tide was out, shooting snippets along the surf-line at high water or rabbits on the landward side of the marram-covered dunes, was ever an irresistible attraction. Also, eight miles out at sea were the dreaded Hasbro' quicksands which have swallowed up hundreds of gallant ships, sucking them down until even the tops of their masts disappeared. Sometimes, however, after striking the sands a vessel would be fortunate enough to get off again, though generally damaged and leaking badly, when she would make all sail for the beach; and I have on one day seen three wrecks lying within a mile of each other.

For this reason Palling boasted a large life-saving station, manned by a company of forty men, called 'beachmen', who, provided with two life-boats and several fast-sailing yawls, did such excellent work in saving life that in those days they stood second in the world's record.

They had a watch-house overlooking the sea, as well as

a look-out in the shape of a square box perched on the top of a fifty-foot spar, by which means a telescopic view of the sands was obtainable.

Also, there was a coastguard station in the charge of a petty officer and four or five jolly tars, and they too had a small life-boat, presented by a local resident, as well as a rocket apparatus and cart, supplied by the Board of Trade.

The trim station, together with a fine flag-staff and a brass mortar eighteen inches long by six inches at the muzzle, and bearing the date 1806 beneath the royal initials G.R. surmounted by the crown, was at that time on top of the dunes, so that the coastguard on watch could bring his telescope to bear on every passing sail, and whenever he, or the beachmen from their look-out, spied a vessel flying signals of distress, or the boom of minute guns from the lightship moored off Hasbro' sands told of a ship ashore there, the mortar would be fired twice, to summon beachmen from their ordinary occupations of ploughing, fishing, etc., to man the life-boat; and as the rule was that he who failed to at least touch the boat before her departure should not share in any salvage money she might earn, every man of the company left whatever he was doing the moment he heard the mortar's roar and rushed to the boat.

A new life-boat, *The British Workman*, had just arrived, and was to be christened by the then Earl of Shaftesbury, the great philanthropist. The matter had been talked of for so long that when the great day actually did come I had forgotten all about it, and not until I suddenly found myself at home alone with the old housekeeper, all other members of the household having mysteriously vanished, did I begin to suspect that doings must be somewhere afoot and at which my attendance had been purposely dispensed with.

While wandering forlornly about the grounds, the old sou'wester of my village friend 'Lum' suddenly appeared at a hole in the hedge.

'Aient yow agoin' t' Pallin' t' see th' new life-boat larnched? Ye' pa and ye' ma an' all on 'em ha' gone drivin' this half-hour an' more. There fare t' be rare goin's on there.'

I realized in a flash, and with feelings of deep wrath, the injustice to which I had so nearly fallen a victim. To crawl under the front gate and join Lum was the work of a few seconds, when we started off at a smart trot through the village, collecting several other urchins as we went.

It was a lovely day, and many objects of interest claimed attention. A wasp's nest in the parish pound delayed our march until two of us got stung. In ditches on either side of the Causeway or 'Cancer' leading across the marshes, numerous water-rats had to be stoned, which excellent sport was greatly enhanced by much splashing of water and mud. Over a blackbird's nest Lum and I came to blows, by which means the brim was all but detached from my straw hat, and it was only the appearance of a 'fower-wheeler an' tu hosses' that caused hostilities to be laid aside so that we might hang on behind; in which manner we travelled, smothered in dust, till near our journey's end, when a few smart cuts from the coachman's whip caused us to abandon further carriage exercise. We were, however, close to the beach, and though wet, dirty and dishevelled, pursued the 'fower-wheeler' like a pack of hounds beneath a triumphal arch of evergreens bearing the legend in white cotton-wool: 'God bless the Earl of Shaftesbury,' which Lum said was 'up to snuff,' until the vehicle pulled up at the foot of the sand dunes, where a great crowd of smart people had congregated.

A tall, sedate-looking gentleman had just descended from the carriage, and was walking with father up the 'gap' towards the coastguard station as I caught up and gave father's coat-tail a good tug, which made him look round, when he exclaimed with a horrified stare: 'Go away, you dirty little ragamuffin'; but I didn't, and then father laughed and held out his hand, which I caught hold of, and he helped me up the hill, while the sedate gentleman, who had iron-grey side-whiskers, looked amused about something, for I could see him quite well through the broken rim of my hat; and so we three walked together up the hill through a lane of nice people all bowing and waving their hats, though some laughed and looked amused, which I thought rather funny, until we came to the station, where the coastguards all held up their guns and the officer drew his sword.

After that father and mother and the tall gentleman, who, I got to understand, was the Earl of Shaftesbury, though he looked just like other people, and many others had lunch at a very long table in the life-boat shed. I peeped in at the door and could see all kinds of nice things: cold tongues, chickens, pineapples, jellies, cakes and flowers. They stayed there an awful long time, eating and drinking and laughing, besides standing up and talking in turns and then cheering. At last, however, they finished and came out, when I went in, and had a splendid lunch, sitting at the long table all by myself, and holding up all kinds of nice things to poor Lum and the others, who looked hungrily through a big crack in the door but dare not come in because of a coastguard, who, though very kind to me, did not seem to like them.

When I had quite finished, I strolled pleasantly down to the beach, and saw the new life-boat, with some ladies and gentlemen on board, being launched. She had only just got through the breakers, however, when something seemed to be amiss, for she put back to the beach, and then I saw mamma, who I had always heard was a wretched sailor, being carried ashore in a state of collapse by two life-boatmen, the spectacle causing me a feeling of satisfaction that my wrongs were being fully redressed: which is the last thing I can remember of that glorious day.

CHAPTER II

Spring

CLOTHES were comparatively useless, for no matter how many might be worn, the roaring, biting east wind, straight from the German Ocean, would go through them like a needle, chilling one to the very bone, and pointing the well-known doggerel—

> *When the wind is in the East,*
> *It's neither good for man nor beast—*

by nipping and drying up any precocious efforts of vegetation, as well as by reducing the average height of the natives, for every one sunk his head into his shoulders and went about moaning and hunched up and complaining that 'the wind's suffen stingy', although the ultimate benefit derived must have been enormous, since a local saying had it that 'March dust was worth a guinea a bushel.' It may have been, perhaps still is; and cheap at the price – seeing what has to be endured to get it.

Presently, however, breezes from the south and west would waft an instantaneous transformation, as if releasing the pent-up joy of spring.

Skylarks singing their loudest out of sheer delight would mount and mount from every field until lost to sight, still singing, in the cloudless blue, and then, tired, would fold their wings and reappear like falling stones till within a few yards of the ground, when, with an upward sweep, they would gently glide to nesting mates.

Thrushes and blackbirds innumerable poured forth sweet songs of praise from every hedgerow, partridges uttered their vibrant calls, hares and rabbits fearlessly romped and made merry in the young wheat, while in marshlands by the Broad the drumming of snipe, the whistle of redshanks and the plaint of peewits would be almost incessant, and o'er the whole countryside, by night as well as by day, would float the mellow note of the cuckoo, whose annual flittings are thus accurately, if ungrammatically, summed up:

> *April, come he will.*
> *May, he sing all day.*
> *June, he lose his tune.*
> *July, away he fly.*

All Nature was awakening: peace, joy, and the promise of life over all.

My brothers and I, like the rest of things, felt the call of spring, and though in turn kite-flying, hoops, tops and marbles briefly held sway, we were far more interested in birds-nesting, in gardening, fishing, and the care of our numerous live stock.

I remember one lovely spring morning when a warm, strong westerly breeze drove fleecy clouds across the sun so that their shadows could be seen racing over fields, while grass and wheatlands heaved with wind-blown billows of sheen and sombre. The hedges were thick with fresh, green leaves; primroses peeped in thousands from every bank; and the voices of all Nature's lesser folk rang loud in praise from every bush and tuft of grass.

Boys are thoughtless wretches, and in such a garden of

peace we spent the day, collecting scores of eggs of various kinds. Our own grounds only were immune, for although they swarmed with song-birds who stole most of the fruit, father did not wish either them or their nests molested; and what father wished was law, for his sweet, unselfish nature claimed from us an obedience such as no martinet could have enforced.

First honours fell to me through being the smallest, for a tomtit's nest having been discovered in a hole in an old elm stump, and not one of the others after much trying being able to squeeze his hand in, I was hoisted up on Harold's shoulders and succeeded in gradually fishing out a dozen tiny round eggs.

Next, Bob spied a fulfer's nest in the fork of an oak, and, before raising the alarm, had swarmed up and taken possession of two beautiful freckled eggs, but having put them into his mouth for convenience when descending the tree, one unfortunately got broken, though not wasted, for, after spitting out the shell, he pronounced the flavour to be excellent. Of blackbirds' and mavises' eggs we secured any number, and also a few each of goolers', spinks', blackcaps', hedgers' and pickcheeses'.

Before starting homewards we lay down a while in the long, cool grass of a shady loke to count our spoil. I forget the total number, but each of us had his cap about half full as we marched in triumph to the gun-room, where the afternoon was spent in making a birds'-egg custard, which, instead of turning out white after prolonged baking in a Dutch oven, had an angry, bloodshot appearance – due, doubtless, to many of the eggs being sat on, but which we nevertheless devoured with great gusto.

On certain marshes around the Broad, green plovers or

'peewits' always nested, and as their eggs when hard boiled and cold are transparent delicacies much prized by epicures, at prices ranging from fourpence to tenpence per egg, it was part of Old Tom's business to collect as many as possible for his eager clients, and oftentimes as a privileged guest I would accompany Grandson Albert on these egging expeditions.

Having quanted across the Broad to Stony Bank in one of the gun-punts, and made her fast to a large boulder, we would slowly and systematically walk up and down marsh after marsh, searching with our eyes every foot of ground for the nests, which, although lying quite in the open and devoid of all cover, being in fact only rough holes or dips in the peaty soil, were extremely difficult to discover, especially as the brown-mottled eggs exactly matched in colour both nest and surroundings, this very simplicity being Nature's safeguard against marauding foes.

When anywhere in the neighbourhood of a nest, the peewits would swoop close round us with loud cries, sometimes even falling to the ground and dragging themselves along as though wounded, in order to lure us in pursuit and so away from their precious eggs. How brave they were, and now clever! But it was all thrown away on Albert, who, apostrophizing them viciously as 'ole warmin', only redoubled his wariness, until presently coming to a standstill, he would call me to him and ask if I could see the nest, which, although perhaps within a yard of me, I often failed to do for some time. The clutch of eggs generally numbered three or four, and they were always symmetrically arranged small ends together, in which position they could neither roll apart nor out of the nest. Moreover, as a consequence of such arrangement they occupied the smallest space possible, and were therefore more easily covered by the bird.

Many other kinds of nests we also saw and examined, but seldom took the eggs, they being of no particular market value.

Coots nested in great numbers amongst the dense reeds which fringed the Broad. Their nests were composed of dry reeds and leaves heaped together in apparent confusion, but in reality placed with consummate skill, for, on close examination, the lower part of each structure was found to possess the qualities of a raft, rising and falling with high or low water, and yet held in position through having been carefully woven about several thick, straight-growing reeds, albeit loosely enough to allow these reeds free vertical play, and it was on this safely anchored, floating platform that the actual nest was built, well above the reach of water. The average clutch numbers from eight to ten eggs of an inconspicuous brown colour, thickly mottled with tiny black spots, while the period of incubation is about four weeks. Young coots are the funniest little customers imaginable, resembling tiny balls of red and multi-coloured fluff, all paddling about with tremendous vigour and in most independent fashion, which leads to many of them being seized and eaten by pike, rats, and marsh harriers.

The coot itself is a remarkable bird. It can hardly be said to have feathers, but rather hair, like the cassowary, and its skin, lined with masses of oily fat, can be detached with great ease, showing its flesh to be almost the colour of mahogany. The hard, white shield on its head, showing up so conspicuously against its grey-black plumage, gives it quite a clerical look, while its feet are only partly webbed, having two or three oval-shaped paddles on each toe. It is a very hardy, fierce, and courageous bird, armed with strong, sharp bill and claws, with which I have known it seize a tame duck that had ventured near its nest and peck in its brains in a few seconds. During mating and nesting season they fight amongst themselves in most ferocious and deadly manner.

The loon or great crested grebe was fairly common on the Broad, where one could generally be seen swimming about by itself in a very independent and picturesque sort of way. It was a wonderful diver and rarely took wing, for although we frequently gave chase when out sailing, it would first swim off at a great pace, with long neck very erect, and tufted, cobra-like head turning quickly from side to side; then, as we drew near, its body would gradually sink and sink until quite submerged and lost to sight, though the erect neck and twisting head would continue cutting through the water as quickly as ever, presenting a most queer spectacle, until in a flash, it had vanished altogether.

Sailing straight on to where we judged the bird would come up, it generally calmly reappeared a hundred yards or so dead astern, having passed under the boat, or a like distance on either side, showing that while diving it could, by either sight, sound, or some other sense, as easily keep track of the boat's position as when swimming on the surface.

I may safely say that no novice could spot a loon's nest.

In thick reed-beds there are always 'lumps' of old, decaying reeds from the previous season's growth, and a loon builds a nest exactly resembling one of these, and as no eggs are ever visible, there is nothing by which to distinguish one lump from another.

On reaching a nest, I have been able to tell, from a string of air-bubbles and stirred-up mud, that the old bird had just dived off it, though I had seen or heard nothing, while apparently there were no eggs. On close examination, however, it will *always* be found that a covering of reed leaves and water-weeds has been hastily drawn over them, which not only serves to conceal, but also to maintain warmth during the owner's absence.

When danger threatens, a baby loon will get on to the mother's back, and, holding on with its bill to her feathers, be carried by long dives into safety.

Of all birds I think I would rather be a swan, as apart from their longevity and graceful beauty, they lead such dignified, clean lives.

There were scores on the Broad, all finding their own living, but all pinioned to prevent flight, and branded on the web or bill as belonging to a lord of some manor. They live to a great age, it is said to close upon a hundred years. As cygnets they are a drab colour, only attaining to pure white when full grown.

The male bird chooses a mate for life, keeping true to and defending her with every mark of deep affection.

Female birds do not appear to lay until they are several years old, perhaps three to five, and then at first only four or five eggs, which is the reason why a brood of one or two is so frequently seen, families of six or seven betokening middle-aged pairs.

Quite young cygnets, when tired with swimming, will scramble up on the backs of their parents, and be so borne along in regal state.

The nests are of coarse reeds roughly piled up on any dry patch of land by the water's edge, on floating sedge, or even in shallow water.

While the female bird is sitting, the male seldom loses sight of the nest, and the moment a boat approaches too close, uttering angry 'r-r-ronks' he will rush back with outstretched neck and wings beating frantically in vain attempts to fly, and, scrambling on to the nest, will stand over his mate, often with one protecting foot on her back, prepared to die in defence of his own.

Standing thus, a good four to five feet in height, with anger-ruffled feathers, strong wings lifted ready to strike, and hissing fiercely through open bill, he presents a very formidable appearance, while every now and then, with sudden lowering of the head, he will gently touch his mate sitting tight on the treasured eggs, as though to hearten and reassure her: the picture of a true and gallant knight.

Amongst themselves, male swans at times fight fiercely. The quarrel generally begins through one bird approaching too near the mate or nest of another, whereupon he is pursued by the lawful owner until he escape or they come to close quarters, when, with ruffled feathers, they will circle round and round each other, almost touching, for hours, and oftentimes without coming to actual blows. If, however, they do happen to touch, battle is instantaneous, and will only cease on one of them taking to flight.

As in other communities, death sometimes robs a swan of his mate, when, apparently almost demented through grief, he will frequently act in the strangest manner, wandering about by himself in all kinds of unexpected, out-of-the-way places.

If big and strong, he occasionally degenerates into such

a bully that all the others are terrified by him, for not only will he furiously attack another swan to which he has taken a dislike, but will relentlessly pursue and finally drown his exhausted victim.

Every year, before the cygnets were half grown and still unable to fly, Old Tom made it a great business to mark and pinion them, and these expeditions were highly exciting.

Two flat-bottomed boats were enough, the object being to first drive a whole family close to the shore or into a small creek, and then interposing one boat between the cygnets and the old birds, beat off the furious attacks of the latter with quants, while Old Tom with a landing-net scooped the young ones into his boat, where they seemed quite helpless, then with his knife quickly snicking off from each the first joint of one wing, and piercing a distinguishing slit in the web of one foot, threw them one by one back into the water, when they swam off with their excited parents, none, apparently, any the worse for such rough usage.

It was a hot ten minutes, for the old birds in desperate attempts to rejoin their young would rush at the intervening boat and try to get into it, while striking heavy blows at us with their powerful wings; but Albert was in his element, and either by thrusting the fork of the quant against their necks would push them underwater all doubled up, or would deal them such blows that I quite expected they would be killed. I also had a quant, and laid about me with a will, though was so excited that beyond splashing every one till drenched, I did not seem to accomplish much; but it was rare fun.

These snow-white swans, with but few exceptions,

have an almost ideal existence, and seem to so thoroughly enjoy life, as they glide leisurely over the clear waters, having merely to dip their long, graceful necks to feed on an inexhaustible supply of luscious weed growing two or three feet below the surface.

In those winters when the Broad was frozen over for several weeks, they might have been hard put to it, but that Old Tom always had large places called 'wakes' kept open for them by breaking the ice.

Of enemies they have none, except that on two occasions within my recollection they were attacked by a large eagle, which is an extremely rare visitor. Albert was a witness of both attacks, made at an interval of several years.

On each occasion the eagle hovered with outstretched talons close over a swan, but before it could strike, the terrified swan dived, and by repeating this manoeuvre with great rapidity, eventually escaped to the reeds, the baffled eagle almost immediately disappearing. This is all the more curious since, during the many years in which I could daily observe these swans, I do not remember ever having seen one dive.

Several kinds of hawks frequented the marshes, and on one occasion a nest containing two half-fledged buzzards was found, of which my brothers purchased one for a shilling, while the village innkeeper, Sam Brush, took the other at a like figure.

Our buzzard, which we christened 'Ben', grew and throve amazingly, hopping about quite contentedly amongst the fowls, getting his feathers.

Every day my brothers would shoot two or three sparrows, which he devoured ravenously, and when able

B

to fly, being allowed full liberty, the report of the gun, or the calling of 'Ben, Ben,' would bring him instantly, and it was a beautiful sight to see him swoop, talons extended, and snatch with unerring aim a sparrow or starling from my brother's outstretched hand, when, carrying it off to a peaked end of the old tithe barn, and pinning his prize down with powerful claws, he would tear off luscious strips with scythe-edged beak and greedily gulp them down.

It was always the same end of the barn, and after a meal he would sit there immovable for hours, rain or fine. It was his eyrie, whitened with bird feathers and bleaching bones, and our big hawk on his homely watch-tower soon became one of the sights of the neighbourhood.

The following spring Ben suddenly disappeared, and although we watched during long months, we never saw him again. He was reported to have been seen at a great height, still mounting and mounting until lost to view; which may have been true, for in spring he would certainly seek a mate, even if the quest carried him to other lands. On the other hand, being so tame, he would run great risk of being shot while enjoying his daily hunting in any distant part of our own neighbourhood.

The number of beautiful birds frequenting this part of East Anglia was extraordinary, for besides the usual upland kinds such as wild pigeons, blackbirds, partridges and robins, there were the marsh birds, such as snipe, redshanks, reed-pheasants and herons; the fresh-water birds, such as loons, coots, wild-duck and swans; and the sea-birds, such as stonerunners and endless varieties of gulls; in addition to all of which many birds of passage belonging to one or other of these four categories seemed to come and go the whole year round.

In spring and summer cuckoos, martins and swallows abounded. Standing on the beach in autumn, Danish crows, larks, linnets and fieldfare could be seen struggling slowly in from the north-east, flying low over the sea, and then, tired out, alighting immediately on gaining the landward side of the dunes; while in winter wild geese and wild swans, frozen out of their customary haunts in Northern Europe, were sure heralds of intense cold.

My own observations were merely those of a child, prompted solely by love of outdoor life and a keen interest in the lesser folk generally, but to any desirous of making a systematic and scientific study of bird-life, probably no district within the British Isles can offer so many opportunities.

Throughout the nineteenth century the parish of Great Waxham was never known to contain a population of more than forty souls, all told, and could neither boast of an inn nor the usual village shop,

In dim, primeval days things must have been on a much grander scale, for there was once a Little Waxham, which, however, the sea incontinently swallowed up several hundreds of years ago, leaving the impoverished senior partner, as it were, to battle alone with an unsympathetic world, so that, protected by lofty sand dunes from further attack by its ancient enemy, the sea, Great Waxham, though sorely stricken, still held on.

Its fine old Hall, originally built some miles inland, and honoured by visits from Queen Elizabeth, latterly stood barely two hundred yards from the beach, and had fallen to the status of a partly-inhabited farmhouse, though even so, as if determined not to be totally eclipsed, it boasted possession of the largest barn in Norfolk: a truly enormous structure with thatched roof.

Close to the Hall stands the church, as though clinging to its companion in former greatness, of which, indeed, it probably was the chapel in feudal times.

Only the body of the church, which is small, of irregular shape, and thatched with reeds from the Broad, is in repair, the chancel being in complete ruins and the tower gutted of both bells and belfry, though in later years covered in with a common tile roof.

Oral tradition has it that a French privateer first demolished the chancel with her guns, and then landed a party of men who burned out the belfry and carried off the fallen bells.

This may or may not be true, but the massive stone walls of the chancel, though still standing, have been pierced and shattered in a way very suggestive of heavy gun fire; in fact, I do not see how else they could have been so wrecked in such an out-of-the-way place.

The inside of the tower being quite open from basement to roof, and there being numberless deep holes in the masonry where the ends of beams and joists had formerly rested, pigeons, hawks, and owls had taken possession, the former being in such numbers as to excite the cupidity of myself and two farmer boys who lived close by.

It would have been easy enough to get the church key, and so we felt there was no harm in entering by an unbolted window instead of through the door.

Up the dark circular stairway, built inside the masonry of the tower walls, we groped on all fours, slipping on piles of sticks and refuse from old nests, and deafened by the roar of wing-beats from scores of startled denizens.

At an opening half-way up, where the belfry platform had evidently been, a hideous young owl and two hawk's eggs were secured by creeping out and back along a perilously narrow ledge; but as it was from the rickety roof that our grand plan of campaign was to be put in operation, we continued the ascent.

One of my companions had brought a plough-line concealed under his jacket, and having removed several tiles, they tied it round my waist just below the arms, and started to lower me down to the joist holes where we could see eggs and young pigeons.

During the making of arrangements, all had seemed very simple and safe, but when I found myself dangling over an eighty-foot sheer drop, twisting round and round as the rope tightened out, things took on a very different hue, and having hurriedly stuffed two young pigeons into my pockets, I yelled to my comrades to haul me up again, which they commenced doing, though very slowly and with much grunting.

My legs swinging in space felt painfully cold, the thin rope tightened round me like a vice, both hands were cut and bleeding through frantic attempts to get a purchase on the rough wall, and when at last I did reach the top, it was only by a final desperate effort that I was eventually hauled through the rafters on to the tiles, when we all collapsed for some minutes.

I suspected then, and feel certain now, that I had been within a hair's breadth of disaster, which the least mishap must have precipitated.

We all felt very much cast down at the meagre realization of our lengthy plannings and great expectations, but to their suggestion that I should go down again I turned a callous ear; while on my remarking that it was the turn of one of themselves, it was firmly pointed out that I was by far the youngest, the smallest, and therefore the lightest.

I must own to having been thoroughly scared, and as there seemed nothing more to be done, we presently stole dejectedly away.

The gaunt old Hall, with its attendant ruined church, standing warden-like on the eastern verge of our island kingdom, separated from total destruction by only a narrow line of dunes, and surrounded by its few remaining acres of arable land, desolate marshes and marram-covered sandhills, always suggested to my mind an aged aristocrat fallen upon evil days, for despite neglect and decay, there was ever a dignity about the old place, enhanced by legends of its coach and headless horses, of the tragic ending to an ancient line, and by tales of its ghost and blood-stained floor; while, lulled by ceaseless murmur of the waves and sheltered by the little church in which for more than half a century he ministered as Rector of Great Waxham, my dear father rests by his mother's side.

Happy recollections of my earliest childhood, friendship's remembrance of one who for a brief space revived bygone glories of the Hall, and sweet memories of him at rest in the little churchyard by the sea, all combine to throne that lonely spot midst affection's most cherished souvenirs. Whate'er the future may betide, swept away by the mighty sea or swamped by human flood, Great Waxham, as I have known thee, Hail and Farewell!

CHAPTER III

The Rectory

THE old rectory stood within its own grounds encircled by a thick zareba-like hedge of holly and blackthorn, effectively screening us from the observation of all passers-by in the adjoining lane.

Within this fortress we were a little world unto ourselves.

The house itself was of venerable appearance, with low, tiled roof, and windows of small, lead-framed panes looking out from clusters of tea-roses and fragrant jasmine, while the boughs of graceful larch and stately limes reached out protectively above and around, until the whole building seemed embowered in foliage.

Welcome house-martins yearly built little mud nests beneath the eaves, and were a subject of constant pleasure to us as they swooped gaily to and fro, twittering happily in secure enjoyment of their homes.

In front of the house was an oval grass-plat surrounded with flower-beds wherein fox-gloves, periwinkle, marigolds, daffodils, roses, tulips and endless other old-time favourites bloomed in rich, intermingled profusion, while beyond a barrier of laurels, pink may, laburnum and rhododendrons lay the kitchen-garden stocked with many kinds of fruit-trees and vegetables, all of which brought forth most abundantly in that rich and heavy soil.

On one side of the house, beneath sycamores, elms

and beeches, was a long, shady walk known as the 'Sand Path' owing to its having been thickly covered with white sea-sand, which, besides preventing weeds from growing because of its saltiness, would quickly dry up after rain, and so always ensure to us a place for walking exercise, and there the cemetery of all our deceased pets was instituted. At the back was a meadow called the 'Bleach', while on the other side were the stables and outbuildings, including an old tithe barn with thatched roof, where, in former times, when the parson's tithe was paid in kind, the corn, etc., had been stored.

I have often heard father relate how that, on taking over the living from his predecessor, who resigned after a prolonged incumbency, he was advised always to open the front door at daylight, and if a keg of brandy were on the doorstep, to take it in, and not allow any one to enter the barn for some days as it was being used by the smugglers, who, as soon as all was clear again, would deposit another keg by way of friendly intimation and rent.

In those days this part of the coast was a very favoured landing place for contraband, as once run clear of the beach, it could be easily and safely distributed all over the county by boating it along the rivers and broads. The dash across the beach and over the three miles of marshes was the great risk, so that the parson's barn, as being above suspicion, was in great request, more especially as it was so conveniently near the Broad.

Father would laughingly bemoan 'those good old days', which came to an end, he said, with the establishment of telegraphic communication between England and the Continent, for no sooner did a cargo of brandy, silk, cigars, etc., leave a French port, than informers telegraphed its destination to the English Custom House. with disastrous consequences to the smugglers.

Old Tom Rudd's father had been a smuggler, and many a time have I gazed with admiration on his flint-lock pistols which still adorned the wall of his son's cottage, and listened breathlessly to the oft-repeated tale of how Old Tom as quite a lad had sailed in the lugger, and that when several successful trips and a good bit of money had been made, his father decided to give up the business after one more voyage; and then my heart would sink on being told of the fearful gale which 'blew we right up the Thames till them there Custom House orficers cam aboard an' took the hull lot on us t' jail, arter strippin' orf the silk laäce I had wownd all round me under my cloes.'

Each of us had a small garden wherein we grew cress, radishes, lettuces, and anything else we had a mind to, the early spring finding us full of enthusiasm as to who could raise the best crops.

We had an old gardener rejoicing in the nickname of 'Trickler', from the trickling-like manner of his gait, and besides attending to our own gardens, we were offered every encouragement to show our skill in anything which might serve to lighten his labours, while he smoked a very ancient clay pipe and issued instructions, so that before our enthusiasm cooled down, we had generally saved him from the necessity of doing any but the lightest of jobs for several weeks to come.

We would compete in digging, Trickler urging us on by awarding praise for both quantity and quality, and it was remarkable what a lot of spade-work five lusty boys could do in three or four days. Then we passed through the raspberry bushes, breaking off and carrying away the old canes, topping the young ones with our pocket-knives, tying them up loosely with strands from old cocoa-nut matting, hoeing out the weeds, and finally putting manure over the roots. No wonder we had the finest raspberries in all the countryside.

Gooseberry bushes were no joke, for we were told they must be first thinned out and then trimmed to the shape of a wine-glass, being flat on top, but before such artistic models could be satisfactorily achieved, our hands and fingers were almost torn in pieces.

Currant bushes, rhubarb, strawberry plants, peas, potatoes, and all suchlike items would be mostly attended to before we finally renounced gardening for the time being in favour of some other pastime. It was very healthful exercise, and, under the tuition of Trickler, really taught us much useful knowledge of simple horticulture.

The flowers were tenderly cared for by my mother and sisters, so that, tended by all members of the family, our old-fashioned garden had acquired that individuality and smiling appearance which the work of loving hands can alone call forth. It was in every sense of the word 'a garden of peace'.

Lawn-mowers being still unknown in those remote parts, the oval grass-plat was consequently mown with a scythe once in about every ten days.

It was a scientific piece of work, requiring great skill, and as the handles of the scythe had to be held very low in order to almost shave off the grass, the amount of backache it involved was considerable. It was the most highly-considered job of all, evoking great criticism, and either sixpence or a shilling from father, according to merit.

Trickler was quite a character, with a proneness to strong drink, and besides gardening had unsuccessfully been in turn innkeeper, butcher, drover, sheep-shearer and rat-catcher, though it was in the last capacity that he chiefly held our appreciation, for he knew all about ferrets: how to breed them, how to keep them, and how to use them; in fact, he was something like a ferret himself.

What one of us did, we all did, and so we all kept ferrets: large ones for rabbiting, small ones for ratting; most of them polecat colour, but some white with pink eyes.

The rambling old outbuildings were just the thing for boys, and in some secluded nook or other each kept several evil-smelling ferrets in a large tub turned up on end and covered by a thick lid which was either securely fastened by chain and staple or weighted with heavy stones, for these bloodthirsty little animals are extremely strong and active, and once out, play deadly havoc with poultry and tame rabbits.

The tub was turned out about once a week and some clean wheat straw put in, beneath which the ferrets would make a nest and sleep there the whole time between meals. If barley straw were used, in a few days the ferrets would be covered with ticks.

For food, dead rats, crows and things of that sort were thrown into the tub, and there left till eaten up, while milk or bread and milk was much appreciated. A little pan of water was renewed daily.

On going to the tub, its inmates would all rush out of the straw, and, dancing on hind legs with fore paws clawing at the sides, look hungrily up in expectation of food.

They soon got to know their master, who, if he put the back of his clinched hand slowly and deliberately against their muzzles, would not be bitten, and could then quietly take them in turn by the neck and lift them out. If, however, he snatched at them with his fingers, he would most certainly be instantly bitten, for they are as quick as lightning.

A popular member of the family was a small fox-terrier named 'Marquis', shortened to 'Mark' or 'Marky', who was more or less considered my especial property, for, besides naturally ranking next to me in importance, we had a great fondness for each other's society. Wherever I went, ratting, sailing, or shooting, Marky, by hook or by crook, was sure to be there also.

Finding the church door open one summer Sunday, he trotted briskly up the aisle, was welcomed into our pew, and established himself under my seat.

Out sailing he was a great nuisance, shivering and whining all the time, even on the hottest days, but nevertheless always insisted on coming. We tried leaving him behind, but he would swim and swim after the boat till we had to take him on board to save him from drowning, when he would shake himself all over every one, and immediately commence to whine and shiver and gaze longingly at the shore in the most uncomfortable manner.

If he could by any possibility steal up to my bedroom in the evening, I would find him comfortably in bed under the clothes, where he would stay till morning, when we got up together. Why he was not suffocated I cannot imagine, for he would get right down by my feet, making a capital 'hot bottle'.

Both for ratting and rabbiting he was splendid, being

quick as lightning, and pluck to the backbone, as well as extremely pugnacious with other and bigger dogs.

Either he could understand in great part what we said, or by some particular instinct comprehend our intentions. Soap and warm water were his especial aversion, and if any one remarked in his hearing, 'Marky must be tubbed', he would disappear for the whole day.

I remember one really wonderful instance of this power of understanding.

My brothers and I had arranged for a day's snipe-shooting round the Broad with Geoffrey, and at eight o'clock breakfast we decided to shut up Marky before starting, otherwise he would be sure to follow us, and the marshes being very wet, would make himself a great nuisance.

We were to meet Geoffrey at Old Tom's at half past nine, but as some time was wasted in a vain hunt for Marky, we did not get there till ten, only to discover him sitting in the middle of the road waiting for us.

Geoffrey, having arrived from the opposite direction punctually at half-past nine, was watching for us, when he saw Marky coming along, and, thinking we were close behind, remarked to himself that it would have been better if we had left him at home, and was somewhat surprised when no one else appeared till half an hour later.

In rainy, winter weather we very seldom went to the Broad, and the dog could not possibly have had any clue that we were then about to go there, a distance of almost a mile.

It was a dismal November day, and we tried to leave him on the bank, but he swam after the boat till we had, as usual, to take him on board, and he made himself a general nuisance all day long, splashing round us, yapping when the guns were fired, and whining from the cold; albeit, I was rather proud of his perseverance, grit and true love of sport.

All these detailed qualities may have been very common affairs, but he had one physical peculiarity which I have never yet seen in any other dog, although constantly on the watch for it.

He had the usual shortened tail, carried a little more than upright, but which he always wagged *straight up and down* with great rapidity, and never from side to side. I believe this would have made a showman's fortune.

Close by lived a small farmer and local preacher, with whom my brothers and I were generally at war, mostly because our chickens and pigeons eat his crops, whereon he, being too good-natured to complain to father, took pot-shots at them with an old rusty gun, which was really far more dangerous to himself than to our live stock. Anyhow, it was fair give and take. He may have occasionally bagged an old hen, while we were saved expense in the matter of chicken food.

Fortunately for us, he usually stacked his corn in a corner of the field adjoining the Sand Path, so that, after it had been threshed, there was a beautiful straw stack all ready to hand.

One of us would keep an eye on the farmer's house standing in another corner of the field, while the others commenced burrowing into the stack by pulling out straw, until at the end of a few days we had a regular network of holes by which we could crawl all through the stack, though it was a very suffocating pleasure owing to lack of both air and light, as well as on account of the thick dust, while our fingers were raw and tender from digging them into the sharp straw.

These horizontal galleries the farmer did not so very much mind, although it cannot be said he altogether appreciated our company, but, when after superhuman efforts in suffocating darkness we completed a spiral tunnel leading out at the top of the stack, so that we could use it as a watch-tower whence to command full view of his comings and goings, he was simply furious.

Armed with a formidable ash stick he strode up wrathfully, vowing that every bone in our bodies should be broken for making holes out at the top of the stack to let rain into his straw; but, warned from the watch-tower, we were all safely in our burrows, and greeted his arrival with derisive whistling.

He ranged round and round, striking wildly whenever a whistling head momentarily appeared at the entrance of a hole, only to be immediately 'whistled' from three or four other places.

We gradually tired of this one-sided game, and, seeking a favourable opportunity, by turns made a dash from our holes, across the ditch and over the bank into the security of the Sand Path.

It was close and exciting work, for the farmer was viciously active, and his stick literally 'hummed' through the air at very close quarters, but we all finally got safely over, with the exception of Clem, who had the hole furthest away, and as he was the only one left, there was no one else for our enemy to watch.

In response to our frequent invitations, he at length made a bolt, with the farmer about two yards behind, and in another moment would also have been in safety had not a branch by which he was hauling himself up given way, so that he slid down the bank again, spread out face downwards.

The farmer was in the ditch alongside him, in a good working position, and it sounded very like the rapid beating of a carpet, till poor Clem finally reappeared and toppled over on our side of the bank, whimpering, and in a state of collapse. For weeks he displayed enormous purple weals to thoroughly interested sympathizers.

We possessed a very ancient though well-bred steed, which formerly had been the property of my Lord John Pelham, Bishop of Norwich, and on her we all learned to ride, bareback, and with heels well tucked in.

Being of a sedate nature, the door of her box was generally left open so that she could wander at will between the stable and the Bleach, where most of her time was spent in cropping the rich, sweet grass.

Amongst other toys I happened to possess one of those discordant mouth-organs, and without having the least idea of how to play any tune, I could still keep up an uninterrupted wailing for almost any length of time.

If no one else enjoyed my recitals, the old mare did, for no sooner had I found a comfortable seat in the sun and commenced to discourse, than she would clatter out of the stable and stand over me with cocked ears and muzzle within six inches of the organ for as long as I continued playing. Never before or since have my musical powers met with such flattering appreciation.

Being the only gee amongst so many, there was great competition for mounts, while her good points assumed in our eyes truly magnificent proportions, as her antiquity and decrepitude were but lightly considered or altogether ignored; after the manner of all owners.

As I said before, we rode bareback, for which reason our riding gear only consisted of a bridle with plain snaffle, and a switch, but as the old lady paid no attention to the latter, we were borne along the country lanes at her own pace, usually a very leisurely one.

Well, one day an old spur was unearthed somewhere in the garden, and so rusted that the rowel would not revolve, though one sharp spike was in position.

A grand council of war was immediately held, the thing being to use the spur without father's knowledge, for he certainly would have forbidden it.

To Matt, as being considered the jockey of the party, was finally accorded the honour of first wearing this lethal weapon.

Having tied it firmly on with yards of string, our representative was given a leg up, and departed at a sleepy trot midst murmurs of admiration.

Hardly out of the gate, Matt proceeded to demonstrate his equestrian skill by touching his mount with the spur.

It was a revelation! The old mare evidently knew what spurs were! Bounding high into the air, with body curved away from the spur, she almost unseated her rider, who only just managed to save himself by clinging on with his heels, which of course meant driving the spur well home.

Tail up, head down, and her hatless rider clinging on with hands and heels for dear life, she travelled up the lane at about thirty miles an hour, and we could hear her hoofs striking the hard road till the sound gradually lessened and finally died away in the distance.

An hour later we met Matt with rueful countenance

leading his charger back dead beat, wringing wet, and with a great raw place on her flank where the sharp spike had been at work.

We were all terrified lest father should know, but managed to smuggle her safely into the stable, where she remained a prisoner for nearly two weeks, while the wound was daily dressed with fuller's-earth and black lead, till all trace of the disaster had disappeared.

Matt, on the other hand, could not sit down with any comfort for several days, while the spur was never used again.

Rabbits, chickens, ducks and pigeons we all kept, and occasionally turkeys and geese, but their care is a matter of such common knowledge that it is hardly worth while going into detail.

At one time each of us was the proud possessor of a small pig, necessitating the erection of several sties, at which we all worked feverishly till completed.

First, four stout posts about four feet high were planted at the corners of an oblong, six feet wide by twelve feet in length. Then rough poles were nailed a foot apart to the inward sides of the posts. Next, a foot deep trench was dug from post to post round the sides of the oblong, and thorn faggots placed in it on end, when more rough poles were nailed a foot apart to the outward sides of the posts, which formed a zareba that no ordinary pig would try to get through.

To the top of this structure for about half its length, some cross poles were nailed, on which were laid more thorn faggots surmounted by a goodly pile of straw by way of thatch, weighted down with a few sods: and the structure was complete.

Troughs we made ourselves from empty boxes, while any amount of straw, intended for stable use, could be found in the barn.

The pigs cost about eight shillings each, and as Trickler's verdict was: 'Yow heant tuk no harm, tegither', I suppose they were fairly cheap.

Our object was to *purchase* as little food as possible, feeding the animals on cabbage leaves, potato tops, a few cinders, and 'swill' from the scullery pig-pail, supplemented by cow-weed and dindles gathered daily along the hedgerows, from which expeditions we would return staggering beneath enormous bundles of green-stuff; and finally, when the pigs had grown large enough for fattening, to sell them again for oftentimes more than double their original cost.

A very necessary though rather painful function was ringing them, otherwise they would root the whole place upside down; but for this operation the services of Trickler were always retained.

The 'rings' are of two kinds: actual rings, which, however, are not very good, as the pigs seem always to quickly get rid of them; and nails, specially made by the village blacksmith, very thin and flat, with large, turn-down heads and extremely sharp points.

Trickler would get into the stye dangling a piece of cord with a noose at one end, and having, after much patient manoeuvring, slipped it into the pig's mouth, would draw it tight with a jerk, and give us the loose end to hold. The pig would struggle backwards furiously, uttering the most awful shrieks as the noose tightened round his snout and drew it into a kind of crimson rose, but we would hold on with might and main, while

Trickler, slowly and deliberately getting astride the patient, would firmly close the gaping mouth with his left hand, thereby deadening the ear-splitting yells, and then with his right hand, slowly but firmly push the whole length of a sharp nail up to its turned-down head through the pink rim of poor piggy's snout, and then taking from his pocket a kind of tin-opener, really the stem of an old door key with a slit in it, would roll up the nail from its point to within a quarter of an inch of the turned-down head.

Two or three nails were considered enough, by the pig as well as ourselves, and effectively put a stop to all his entrenchings.

Some of us actually made a small profit on our ventures, but one day when Matt was out we suddenly discovered his pig had died.

Sympathy should have been extended, but such is the force of competition, even in pig-farming, that it was looked upon as rather a good joke, the defunct porker being nailed by his ears to a high wall overlooking the sty, so to await his owner's return, while we others watched the trend of events through chinks in the turnip shed wall.

Matt approached the sty with a bunch of dindles, and, throwing them in, called invitingly: 'Pig, pig, pig! Pig, pig, pig!' but getting no response, made a noise with his mouth in imitation of a pig eating: 'Ts-ch, ts-ch, ts-ch! Ts-ch, ts-ch, ts-ch!' which usually irresistible call being also unanswered, he fairly beamed, for such sound sleep beneath the straw clearly proved how well his animal was 'doing', and, getting into the sty to awaken the sleeping beauty, commenced putting aside the straw with his hand, at first slowly, then quickly, then frantically, till finally standing up and gazing round with a black stare, his eyes encountered the object on the wall.

I had often seen him angry before, but never so absolutely '*wild*', which state of feeling a general titter from behind the turnip shed wall did nothing to assuage, so that, being suddenly mindful of things to be done indoors, I somewhat hastily withdrew.

A good-sized outhouse with window, fire-place and carpenter's bench, served as gun-room, and this we considered our especial domain.

There were three guns, all muzzle-loaders: father's old double-barrel, a long single-barrel with cheek-pad on the stock because she kicked, and a short single-barrel, daily quarrelled over by Clem and Bob.

Father did not present me with a gun till my ninth birthday, so that in earlier times I was dependent for any shooting on the good-will of others, which goodwill had to be dearly purchased.

For anything that I could do, run errands, cut wads out of cardboard or book-covers, tend ferrets or pigs, there was only one payment – so many shots – and payment was never better or more eagerly earned, with the result that while still quite a nipper, I could knock over a sparrow on the wing with the best of them.

The question may already have occurred to some as to what we did by way of lessons. Well, not a very great deal.

Three miles distant there lived an old-time Dominie, very small and slight and with rather a stoop. He wore dingy black clothes, a stock, an ancient top hat, took an enormous quantity of snuff, was a fierce, unsympathetic Radical, had long grey hair and beard, and in face bore a striking resemblance to the portraits of Charles Dickens, while in speech he was slow, pedantic, 'acidulous'.

To this fount of knowledge we were supposed to make a daily pilgrimage, each carrying his lunch and books in a bag, and there be 'inculcated with the rudiments of a sound education'.

English grammar was his strong point, and we learned grammar on the road there, we had a prolonged grammar lesson each morning, a grammar lesson every afternoon, and had grammar to learn in the evening. 'Grammar', he daily informed us, 'being the art of speaking and writing correctly'.

To the anxious inquiries of my dear mother as to my capabilities, progress, and general deportment, I overheard his cheering reply that I was 'born to be hung'.

He had a lady-housekeeper of the early Victorian stamp, with little side curls, crinoline, and a warm, kind heart. She was accounted very clever and accomplished, writing a beautiful hand, being a brilliant pianist, a wonderful maker of wax flowers and sea-shells, and a gifted worker in embroideries.

What types they both were, and how thankful I am to have known them, if only to more fully appreciate the characters of Dickens!

CHAPTER IV
Youth

GRANDSON ALBERT, who, from being as meek and quiet as a mouse with Old Tom at home, became the 'nisiest young warmin as iver wuz' as soon as his grandfather was safely out of ear-shot, when his favourite pastime consisted in running backwards and forwards along the thatched roof of the boat-house, yelling at the top of his voice out of sheer delight at being free from the dreaded tyrant.

We were soon on the field, joyfully adding to the general uproar, while swarming into boats and about the premises with great freedom, till suddenly Grandson Albert took a flying leap from the top of the boat-house on to a pile of litter, exclaiming in a terrified voice: 'Here come my gran'fa, drunk as muck. Be yow a-stirrin' tegither.'

Stir we did, and in ten seconds every one was effectually concealed, while Albert had vaulted, cart-wheel fashion, over the stable-yard gate and was chopping turnips for his life between furtive peeps over the fence at, and excited warnings as to, the approaching tornado: 'Massy upon us! he's a-comin' like bells. Lay yow right squat tegither. Th' ole warmin!'

The sudden stillness about the premises, together with the sound of approaching wheels, instantly brought out Mrs Rudd, who, pale of face and trembling with fright, kept on exclaiming helplessly: 'Massy upon us! God know!

Boy Ollbut, be yow a stirrin'. Massy upon us!' till her lord and master could be seen coming up the bank, 'hallerin' an' yawlin' ' and rolling from side to side in his square cart as the small cob tore along at full gallop, till, pulling up at the gate with a jerk, Old Tom was first thrown on to the pony's back, and then slipped down between the animal and the shaft, where he hung with his feet just off the ground, glaring like a tiger and saying all kinds of things, while Mrs Rudd and Albert worked frantically to undo the harness and set him free.

It could only have been a few seconds, though it seemed an age to me watching from behind an empty tar-barrel, before the cob walked forward and Albert dropped the shaft as though it were red-hot and fled to the hay-house closely followed by Old Tom striking at him with his left hand as he ran, while Mrs Rudd brought up the rear.

The hay-house was separated from the turnip shed by a partition some seven feet high, which Albert scaled like a cat, but which Old Tom was unable to get over, and before he could retrace his steps, Mrs Rudd had banged to the hay-house door and securely fastened it outside, making her husband a prisoner.

The din inside for a few minutes was awful, but it soon subsided, and in a short time stertorian snores proclaimed that the master of the house had found a comfortable bed upon the soft hay.

It was like having caught and caged a lion, so that after hastily collecting at the gate and briefly talking the event over in excited whispers, we all stealthily dispersed, while Old Tom, having had a comfortable and refreshing sleep, would find the hay-house door open when he awoke, so that things would resume their natural course, every one being most careful not to allude in any way to the 'regrettable incident'.

Bathing, or in local parlance 'washing', had a great fascination for us, not only in the bright, clear water well out, but also in the muddy deeks and reed-beds along the shore, for there feathery grasses, bulrushes, freshwater mussels, reed-birds' nests and yellow irises were to be found; besides, the shallow water was far warmer, and it was so nice to come out on to the Hill-common, run up and down in the soft, damp grass, and dry in the sun; while the Bank residents had become so accustomed to seeing half a dozen naked boys playing about, that usually they paid no more heed to us than we did to them.

I say usually, for on one occasion when we were all sitting on the garden wall of a retired farmer, basking in the sun, the old gentleman rushed out of the house in great excitement, saying: 'Boys, boys, be off. I have ladies to tea,' whereupon we obligingly slipped down, hopped across the road, dived into the deek, and swam in single file towards the open Broad.

On another occasion Matt, in Nature's garb, was mardling up the dusty road, enjoying a sun bath and gathering blackberries from a garden hedge, when a lanky, dour-looking lass of some fourteen summers charged out with a long stinging nettle.

One look satisfied Matt that safety lay only in flight.

Up the road and across the marsh they flew, Matt, with a terrified look on his face, about four inches ahead of the nettle, and never in my life had I seen him put in better work, for despite bare feet over sharp stones and rough marsh stubble, he reached the water just untouched, and splashing in up to his knees, fell down at full length and paddled out to deep water and safety, while his irate pursuer warned him from the bank that she would 'larn him wit to come a-stealin' her blegberries, that she would'.

Even after this defeat, it was hard work to tear ourselves away, so that having donned both shirts and neckties we yet spent a considerable time paddling, until Matt, venturing in too far, got his shirt-tails all wet, when, in order to avoid catching cold, he just tore them off.

Still he could not dress and go, but becoming reckless, got his shirt wet again and had to tear off another strip all round; then again and again, till eventually there was, nothing left but just the neck-band and the sleeves, though when at length he did get his clothes on, no one would ever have suspected it.

The many torn-off strips we carefully carried home for gun cleaning.

Old Tom's cob was a wonderful animal of great age, and, like ourselves, almost amphibious, for when not at work she roamed at will round the edges of the Broad, fording or swimming deeks, and wading in up to her shoulders to crop the tender young rushes; which style of life apparently suited her uncommonly well, for until long past twenty, she still looked young, with legs like steel bars, as well as being full of life and strength.

Again, like ourselves, she thoroughly understood her master and his ways, for although time after time she brought him home, overpowered by Bacchus, tearing at full gallop round dangerous corners and with reins loose on her back, never once was there a collision or an upset, and having pulled up at the gate with a jerk, Old Tom might be shot out on to her back, or slip down between her and the shaft, she would stand perfectly still until unharnessed and set free to forage for herself.

Old Tom, on the other hand, was very fond of the cob in his rough and rasping way, and uncommonly particular as to her appearance.

Well, Albert's younger brother Jethro had also just come to live with his grandparents, and one day when 'gran'fa wuz on ter Broad' this youngster started to trim the cob's beautiful, thick, flowing tail with a reap hook or sickle, in order to make it look smart, like Squire Postle's hack.

He first cut it off square, as short as possible, which made it bunch out like a cabbage, so that a good deal of thinning out was necessary. It was very difficult, however, to achieve a smooth and even appearance, and poor Jethro, getting scared at what he had done, worked at it the whole afternoon, snicking off a few hairs here and a tuft there, till finally, to his horror, there was almost nothing left but the bare stump.

Next morning Old Tom was taking some plover's eggs to a country house about ten miles distant, and at the start Jethro was able to conceal the stump with a rug till his grandfather was seated, when the splash-board intervened, and it was only on arrival at his destination that the inquiry of a grinning groom: 'What have you done to the pony's tail, Rudd?' caused Old Tom to discover the true state of affairs.

The return journey was made at full gallop and without stopping at a single wayside inn, and what eventually happened to Jethro I shall not explain, but to this day if you ask him: 'Who cut the pony's tail?' he will shake his head and change colour.

Immediately in front of Old Tom's cottage was a small creek with landing-place or staithe, where the duck-punts and other craft used to lie when not in the boat-houses.

This creek or 'deek' was in the form of a right angle, and some forty yards long by only about six feet broad at the extreme end, though gradually widening to perhaps thirty feet where it opened into the Broad. In depth it was about four feet: two feet water and two feet thick black mud.

Beginning at the narrow end, we would in turn all take a short run and jump across it with ease, then over a wider place a little higher up, and so on, until one by one we surpassed our limit, failed to reach the opposite bank, and went in.

It was capital exercise and rare fun, though ruinous to our white duck trousers, which, despite frequent washing, gradually took on a permanent, coffee-coloured hue.

The Rarverand was a frequent visitor to the Broad in those days, and no sooner did we espy his majestic figure approaching through the fields, than we set to work jumping across the deek with all our might.

The result was always the same. He would stride up in a lordly way and inquire in his mellow, resonant voice: 'Why are you boys not at school?' to which, being the youngest, I was generally pushed forward to explain that the weather was too fine.

'Oh, too fine! Too fine, is it? Well, what the world's coming to I don't know! 'Pon my word! Too fine, eh?' and then he would go off into a rich, melodious laugh which took into his confidence and delighted the little crowd of hangers-on by which he was already surrounded.

'Oh, too fine, is it? Too fine! Well, I see you are learning to jump, at all events. Now, then, I wonder if any of you can jump over here,' indicating a place about eight feet wide.

Over we flew like a string of hunters.

'Not so bad – not so bad! Now, how about this?' choosing a ten-foot jump.

At it we dashed, but probably being beyond my powers, I would fail to reach the further shore and disappear beneath the stagnant wave, though only for a moment, crawling out black as a nigger from a coating of mud, which diffused a full-flavoured bouquet.

This was what the Rarverand was waiting for.

'Well done, little 'un!' he would roar, with a burst of laughter and tossing me either a sixpence or a shilling. 'A chip of the old block, eh? Haw, Haw, Haw!'

'Now, then, you others', he would add, choosing in succession jumps of twelve, fourteen, fifteen feet, and so on, till we had all had a ducking and earned a reward; though personally, when once wet and the greed of gain on me, I gleefully followed through the widest places, thereby gaining great *kudos* and as much as half a crown in the afternoon.

At other times we would run at the jump with a quant, planting it in the thick, deep mud and vaulting over, which required a good deal of skill and practice, though the knack being once acquired, almost double the distance could be covered. My elder brothers were very expert, and I have repeatedly seen them clear the deek at its widest part.

Our greatest joy was to get some stranger, a Londoner for preference, and by jumping over wide places with the quant, so fire his zeal, that eventually he would himself essay to jump over a narrow place.

Of course he would hold the quant all wrong, and make several false starts, exclaiming all the while he was sure he would go in, to which, by way of encouragement, we would vehemently declare he certainly would not. Meanwhile, we all gathered round in an innocent manner, each concealing a brick or a clod behind his back, so that when at length the stranger did make a dash at it, a shower of missiles into the water just in front of him would raise such a splash that he invariably lost his head, and either let go the quant altogether, or planted it too far in advance, with the inevitable result that he at once went head over heels into the deek, from which a mud-covered object would presently crawl to a merciless accompaniment of jeers and convulsive laughter.

Old Tom had a muzzle-loading swivel duck gun of great antiquity, but which we regarded in much the same light as we did its owner: with feelings of awe and veneration.

In its youthful days it had been a flint-lock, but marching with the times, it had been converted by the local blacksmith into a percussion cap weapon, the trigger being about as delicate as a man's thumb, and the hammer something like a bed-key. The stock was a portly, worm-eaten piece of furniture, and the barrel, while holding a strong bend upwards, had no sight. The bore was about No. 2, I should guess, and the entire length of the gun from six to seven feet, while to about the middle of it a thick iron pin or swivel was firmly welded.

In the duck-punt was a heavy oak cross-beam, securely clamped to either side of the boat, with an iron-plated socket in the middle.

The weapon was mounted by placing the iron pin into

this socket, which arrangement threw all the recoil on to the oak beam, while the gun, balancing on the swivel, could be easily trained from side to side, as well as slightly raised or depressed.

The regulation charge for this Woolwich Infant was twenty drachms of powder and eight ounces of swan-shot.

In bitter winter weather with stock-ice forming below water and hanging on to the oars and quant like liquid glass, and with sleet and snow driving before a howling nor'-easter, Old Tom, muffled up in seal-skin cap, thick blue guernsey, heavy woollen scarf, crotch boots and oilies, would put out and creep along the windward shore until he spotted a flock of mallard, 'pokers', or wild geese on the water to leeward, when, lying face downwards along the bottom of the punt with eyes just above the gunnel, one hand working a single scull over the side, and the other hand on the trigger, he would bear down before the wind on his prey, until the moment when they began to rise he would loosen into them the eight ounces of swan-shot.

At times he made splendid bags, the best I have heard him state being thirty-three mallard and pokers at one shot; though in mild, open winters, when the wild-fowl were not frozen out of their haunts in the salt swamps along the coasts of Denmark and Holland, he sometimes never even fired a shot, so that the duck-punt, with the big gun mounted and loaded in readiness, would lie majestically in the boat-house for weeks, while Old Tom would sit at home in his arm-chair, and through the open door continually scan the surface of the Broad with field-glasses in hopes of detecting the longed-for fowl.

Just how it happened I never knew, but the attraction of the 'sweervle' evidently proved too strong for Harold, who, watching his opportunity, secretly crept into the punt and was doubtless examining with guilty joy the mighty weapon, when suddenly it blazed off with a terrific roar, blowing out the end of the boathouse and sweeping the Bank with its eight ounces of swan-shot.

That no one was killed must be ascribed to the lucky accident that no one within half a mile happened to be in the line of fire.

Quick, was the word. Harold disappeared as if by magic, so that Old Tom, on rushing to the scene, found nothing but a smoking gun and damaged boat-house; and I doubt if to the end of his days he ever knew who the culprit really was, though, doubtless, he laid the blame pretty close to where it belonged. Anyhow, neither business nor pleasure took any of us down to the Broad for several weeks.

Picnics to the beach were always a source of great enjoyment, and I remember one occasion well when several of my brothers and sisters, myself and two maids, started off for the day.

The lunch-basket and as many of us as possible were stowed in the old-fashioned gig, while the remainder either ran or hung on behind till their turns came for a lift, when places were exchanged with those who had already taken their share of carriage exercise.

In due course the cavalcade reached its destination, when our chariot and ancient gee having been put up at the village inn, we all made for the beach, carrying the lunch-basket with us, but finding it very heavy, we presently concealed it amongst the marram-covered sand-hills and continued our walk, intending to return later on.

It was lovely by the sea, so that bathing, paddling,

gathering sea anemones, star-fish, shells, thunderbolts, seaweed, pieces of bamboo, and many other treasures cast up by the waves, we had covered a good two miles before realizing that it was time for lunch, to get which, however, an equally long walk back was necessary.

By this time one of the maids had disappeared in the direction of her 'follower's' cottage, while my youngest sister, being quite tired out, required all the attention of the other.

A halt having been come to, a council of war decided that it was useless for all to trudge back when one alone could fetch the basket.

This was sound reasoning, but who was to be the one?

My sisters were quite exhausted, or pretended to be, while my brothers having brought a gun, declared they could not spare the time, as there were rabbits on that particular part of the sand-hills; and so, to my dismay and indignation, I was singled out as being the youngest of the boys to fag for the whole party.

I flatly refused to go, and, lying on my back, for a time kept all at bay by vigorous kicking, though eventually active pressure from superior numbers told, and I was driven off by blows, threats, and stone-throwing.

Black wrath boiled within me as I crawled back those now seemingly endless two miles.

At length I reached the basket, and whether it was vengeance which prompted me, or whether I was really faint from want of food, I cannot now remember; but the fact remains that instead of shouldering the basket and conveying it to the expectant party, I found myself seated beside it, preparing to enjoy a thoroughly good meal.

The beefsteak pie was excellent, and I really did justice

to it, till a dark cavernous void under the crust was plainly noticeable. Then there was a most delicious custard jelly in a pie-dish, especially brought for my youngest sister, who was not very strong. Of this I managed to consume a good half. Two or three apple puffs rounded off the banquet.

Lunch over, I lay back contentedly in the soft, warm sand, to comfortably think things over for a few minutes before starting:

'It was a long way to carry that heavy basket; a very long way.

'I wonder what they will say when they find out how much I have eaten.

'I don't feel quite easy as to how they will take it.

'In fact, I don't at all like the prospect; and after all, they made me come when I didn't want to, so, why should I—'

The idea came full and strong. Vengeance, reparation and escape from further difficulties – all at one fell swoop!

Trembling with joy and excitement, I filled up the yawning cavern in the beefsteak pie with sand, and in like manner replaced the missing half of the custard, patting them down with my hands to get symmetrical proportions, and then tossing a few handfuls of dry sand into the basket generally, I left things as they stood, and chuckling with guilty joy at the thought that everything in the basket being full of sand nothing would be eatable, started straight off on the four mile walk home, which I reached in time to join with some afternoon callers in a very superior tea, explaining my early return as due to feeling a little tired, and thereby gaining in addition much pleasant sympathy.

About two hours later I watched from the safety of my bedroom window the picnic party's return, and felt justified.

Hunger, exhaustion, impotent wrath, tears — all were there, and what more could grace any conqueror's triumph?

For several days my brothers prowled round about me like troops of Midian, ever watching; but I had suddenly developed an extreme fondness for the society of my parents, who I felt tacitly supported me; and they didn't get a chance, so that to the very end my victory was full and complete.

After harvest, when there was not much doing on the farms, a certain amount of employment was found for regular hands in brushing holls and deeks, or, to use ordinary English, in cutting brambles and grass out of ditches, and trimming down hedges and banks.

The resultant brambles and grass or 'brush' being useless, such was first allowed to dry and then collected into one monster heap in some ploughed field to be duly burnt on the fifth of November, 'bonfire night'.

As far as I can remember, it always poured with rain on bonfire night, but that did not in any way allay the excitement with which we boys watched for those dull, red glares which told where fires had been lit.

From dark till well on towards midnight my brothers and I, together with a mob of village boys, were on the move, taking a bee-line in the rain and inky November darkness from fire to fire, floundering ankle-deep across ploughed fields, scrambling over high banks, and crawling through thick blackthorn hedges, till we were coated with mud, soaked with rain, and steaming with perspiration from our terrific exertions, as well as from the fierce heat of several different fires, for no sooner did one commence to die down, than we left it and started off full cry to any other which was just beginning to show up.

On one occasion our kind-hearted old enemy 'the small farmer and local preacher', who lived close by, had invited quite a number of his flock to an extensive tea, after which, by way of a great treat, they were to set his bonfire alight.

Being so near at hand, we boys had watched with interest this mountain of brush daily growing in size, till at last we almost began to feel that it in some measure belonged to us.

Anyhow, there it now was, waiting to be lit, while the invited guests were taking an inexcusable length of time in finishing their teas, so that having waited at least a full five minutes, we approached it unobserved in the darkness, and, simultaneously applying matches in some half-dozen places, it was very well alight, if not almost burnt out, before we caught sight of several infuriated members of the tea-party advancing rapidly and brandishing thick sticks, which spectacle caused us, uttering whoops of triumph, to melt away into the darkness on a bee-line for the next.

Talking of monkeys, Matt had a great big brute, almost as tall as I then was, a matter of perhaps three feet; leastways, he seemed of great stature to me, for we were deadly enemies.

Where he came from I do not rightly know, but, secured by a chain to the old-fashioned kitchen range, he lived on top of the oven, which had always a pleasantly warm temperature. There was continual trouble.

The kitchen-maid when cleaning the range brushed Ginney's toes for fun, whereon he flew at her, put his arms round her neck, and made his teeth meet through her ear.

I remember the maid howling and screaming, and of course she wanted to leave, till things quieted down again.

Ginney, for that was the beauty's name, put a live kitten into the oven, took lids off the saucepans and with his black fingers picked at their contents. Also, getting a box of matches, he tried to eat the red sulphur heads, till presently one ignited between his teeth, whereon that game palled.

He escaped and was lost in the cornfields for several days, terrifying poor old Judy Hatten, who, seeing him sitting on a stile near her house, rushed all the way back to the village, declaring she had seen the Prince of Darkness, tail and all, 'an' he won't let me pass nowhere'; which may or may not have been anticipating matters. Finally he was recaptured by Matt, though almost dead from starvation.

Coming up stealthily behind, and seizing me by the hair, he nearly shook the life out of me before assistance arrived, for which act of treachery we were, as already stated, deadly enemies.

Whenever he heard me coming along the passage to the kitchen, he would poke his ugly little face round the corner to look, and then draw back, waiting.

By squeezing close to the further wall I could just creep by, though, straining at his chain, Ginney's clutching fingers would come within two or three inches of my legs.

This could not go on, so one day when nobody was about, I heated the dining-room poker red hot, then letting it cool off till it was black, started for the kitchen.

Ginney, ever on the alert, heard me coming, looked round the corner to make sure, and then drew back, waiting.

Holding the poker well in advance, I quickly slid it close past the corner, when, in a flash, Ginney had seized it, though simultaneously he seemed to strike the ceiling, the floor, the oven and everything else within the radius of his chain.

Victory was complete! Ginney kept well up on the oven, cackling and coking in great style, while I paraded unmolested to and fro with my wand of office; and from that day on my supremacy was never again challenged.

Strangely enough, Ginney's only serious burn was on one of his hind feet, and for years afterwards, if any one said to him 'Show us your sore leg', he would instantly poke it out for inspection, in most ludicrous fashion.

The vital question for all was, how to get rid of the beast.

Eventually Matt was induced to present his pet to friend Geoffrey, who took it off in triumph, though only, to our dismay, to return with it in a wheelbarrow about an hour later, saying his father absolutely refused to have a monkey on the premises.

How it was managed I do not know, but Geoffrey's father must have relented, for Ginney went to live at the farm; which brings me to the point I desire to illustrate: how to keep monkeys well and happy in our damp, raw climate.

The end of Ginney's chain was fastened to a cross-beam in an outhouse where several pigs were being fattened, by which means he could roam all over the shed to the length of his tether. He could swing and play amongst the rafters, or, descending hand over hand down his chain, hop about in the straw.

He quickly became good friends with all the pigs, though holding them in complete subjection, and always singling out one as his especial favourite.

Eating the same food as the pigs, barley meal and maize, he and his favourite would dine first, before any of the others were allowed to approach the trough.

Much of his time was spent in sleeping, deep down between two fat pigs, so keeping warm and cosy, though instantly poking up a queer, ugly little face whenever any-one opened the door.

By way of diversion, or shall we say sport, the bristles of each pig were daily counted, or at least inquisitively turned over; for Ginney was aye searching – searching – searching!

In this happy manner the monkey, as a great pet of Geoffrey's father, lived to an honoured old age of a dozen years or so, his only apparent trouble being that annually about three inches of his once extremely long tail withered, drooped, and fell away – like a tale that is told.

The leisured ease of a pig's life is unpleasantly punctu-ated by the occasional putting of rings in his snout, to prevent rooting, until brought to a tragic close when led forth to execution. On all of these occasions the excite-ment and fury of Ginney knew no bounds, and woe betide any molester of his porcine friends that came within reach of those lightning, frantic leaps and gnashing teeth.

Only a monkey, Ginney was ever ready to lay down his life for his friends, although but pigs; and what more could be asked of even mortal, Christian man?

The actual bottom of the Broad was mostly hard clay and gravel, carpeted by a foot-thick layer of lush, sponge-like weed.

As this weed in natural course died down before each succeeding new growth, it was held locally that the Broad would eventually become filled up by accumulations of decayed vegetation – a disaster too awful for contemplation.

In winter work was short on the farms, so that after all hands had returned from herring fishing, a good few idlers would collect on the village green to smoke and yarn between visits to the nearest inn for refreshments and skittles, while dog-fights and bouts at fisticuffs, attended by deafening uproar, were of daily occurrence.

So long as these idlers were unmarried men it was nobody's concern but their own whether or not they could afford to 'play', as the local term had it; but when hungry youngsters had to be fed it was another matter.

It thus happened that every winter a few of this leisured class would 'go a-weedin',' which signified that two 'partners' having secured the use of a large, tarred, flat-bottomed lighter, known as either a 'load boat' or a 'half load boat', according to size, and a couple of four-tined weed rakes, they would rake up weed and mud from the bottom of the Broad, haul it into the lighter, stack it up in big heaps on shore, and eventually sell it at so much a tumbler load for manure.

What attracted me to the scene was the fact that to-gether with the weed and mud numbers of small eels were hauled into the lighter, and it always afforded a certain amount of cold, wet and very dirty sport hunting for those slimy little reptiles amongst the dripping weed or in the thick and highly aromatic water collected at the bottom of the boat.

With rare exceptions, they were too small to be of any use, but the mere fact of being on the Broad, though only aboard a weed-boat and in mid-winter, together with the excitement of the chase, was sufficient inducement; while the pleasure of marching home through the village with one's pockets bulging and quaking from the contortions of a dozen eels, was not to be overlooked.

With the advent of better times, weedin' has ceased, while the game of skittles or nine-pins, as being conducive to drinking and brawling, has been suppressed by law, together with systematic dog-fighting and open pugilistic encounters.

Although only very small eels were hauled into the weed-boats, it did not mean there were no larger ones about. On the contrary, there were any number of all sizes, many running up to four, five, and even six pounds in weight, only those monsters were far too strong, wary and and active to be caught by such simple appliances as weed crooms.

On warm summer evenings after a shower or tampist, when not a breath of air ruffled the Broad's mirror-like surface, whereon tall rushes, osiers and willow trees were reflected with almost startling vividness, and when the water was so clear that every detail of the sponge-like weed at the bottom could be seen for a radius of quite thirty feet, eel darting, or picking, would afford very pleasant sport for a couple of hours or so.

The iron dart or spear then in use was about eight inches in width, with fifteen or twenty sharp, barbed prongs, some seven inches long, a ten-foot wooden shaft completing the weapon.

Standing all but motionless at the extreme end of a flat-bottomed boat, one would silently dip first one end of the dart into the water and then the other, thereby drawing the boat very slowly along, while keeping a sharp look-out on the weeds below.

The least sound or the least jerk to the boat would be fatal, for eels have a very keen sense of hearing, and not one would be seen.

Proceeding, then, with all necessary caution, a waving, ribbon-like object is presently discernible, until silently gliding nearer you make out that it is a good-sized eel, perhaps two feet long and weighing from one to two pounds.

The water being only about three feet deep and as clear as crystal, you see that the eel's head is thrust a few inches into the weeds or mud, probably in search of food, while its tail is the waving, ribbon-like object.

Now is your chance! Bracing yourself up as the boat glides slowly onwards, and holding the dart so as to strike across the eel, you measure the distance, and then thrust with all your might. Instantly drawing back the dart, you will probably find a mass of weeds, together with the eel, impaled on the barbed prongs, from which it can be forced by pressure of the foot, and left to explore at will the bottom of the boat, apparently but little the worse for having been almost cut in two.

As often as not eels at the last instant become aware of their peril, and are off like a flash, the dart bringing back nothing but weeds.

On a good evening I have frequently speared from a dozen to twenty in the hour.

The spear which I have just described is now illegal on the score of cruelty, though another pattern, shaped very like Britannia's trident, and having five flat, barbed prongs, each about two inches wide, is allowed. The prongs or teeth of the old spear would pierce clean through an eel, while with the new spear an eel would be held squeezed between the prongs.

Eels are very tenacious of life, and it is a matter of common belief that even after having been chopped up into several lengths, they will not die till sundown. This may be slightly exaggerated, but not much.

It is almost useless trying to kill an eel either with a stick, by cutting its head half off, or by any other method which attacks only one part of its body at a time.

At the end of summer, and mostly by light of the harvest moon, masses of eels hurry down from remotest inland waters to the sea, in order to spawn.

What a scurrying, exciting journey it must be especially as all along the line of march, by way of streams and rivers, systematic traps, in the shape of eel nets, are spread to catch them, until it is really a wonder that any escape to fulfil their mission.

These eel nets are not spread promiscuously, for the right to do so at certain places, called 'eel-sets', has been leased from time immemorial by the different villages or lords of the manor through whose property the river flows, to any one desiring to follow the occupation of eel-catcher.

At opposite points on either side of a river there is a small jetty or landing-stage, made by facing the river bank with stakes firmly driven into the mud. From jetty to jetty a funnel-shaped net of small mesh is spread, totally blocking the river. The funnel gradually narrows down stream until it leads into a succession of hoop-nets, finally terminating in what is called the 'pod'.

Eels running down to the sea and finding the road blocked, naturally enter the funnel in hopes of making a way through.

Once into the hoop-nets there is no chance of escape, retreat being cut off by a clever arrangement of strings, called the 'char' or 'purse', so that, working onwards as far as possible, all victims finally enter the pod, which the eel-catcher bodily detaches at daybreak, the whole of the catch, oftentimes from five to ten stone in weight, being immediately transferred to eel-trunks (large boxes perforated with numerous holes through which water can freely ebb and flow but too small to allow of the eels escaping), and heavy lids being securely padlocked, the trunks can be pushed bodily into deep water, the eels thereby keeping alive and fresh for days, until needed for private customers or the nearest market.

As eels run only at night, the heavy net would be slackened off and allowed to sink several feet during daytime, so as to avoid the keels of passing craft, but at sundown it would be hauled up tight to the stakes until the corks buoying its upper edge floated on the surface, while the lead sinkers attached to its lower edge would rest on the bottom.

As it was always possible that a deep-laden wherry might come along after dark, when in order to avoid having the net either cut in two or torn bodily away, it had to be temporarily lowered while she glided by, as well as owing to the fact that a podful of eels would be a very acceptable prize for any night prowlers, it was necessary that some one should watch the nets all night.

Shelter for these watchers was usually provided in the shape of a cabin-boat.

As wrecks along the sea-coast were so numerous, it naturally followed that at auctions of wreckage a stout ship's boat could oftentimes be purchased for a few shillings, and when a rough cabin had been built on, it could be floated to any set, and there admirably fulfil the requirements of an eel-catcher's shelter.

The whole of Broadland is sprinkled with these Peggotty's huts, either floating alongside the set, or drawn up into a convenient position on the bank.

Old Tom had an eel-set at the Broad's narrow outlet, as well as a cabin-boat, and as either Albert or Jethro would be in command, I was a frequent and welcome visitor, taking the deepest interest in all matters pertaining to eel-catching.

CHAPTER V

Sport

M y elder brothers all having guns, I was brought up in an atmosphere of powder and shot, so that it really is impossible to say when I learned to shoot; in fact, the art was acquired naturally, in much the same manner as learning to walk.

My brothers' three guns were all muzzle-loaders, fired, of course, by means of percussion caps or 'patches'; and, as I said before, they consisted of father's old double-barrel, a long single-barrel with cheek-pad on the stock because she kicked, and a short single-barrel, daily quarrelled over by Clem and Bob.

Our constant anxiety was ammunition, almost every farthing we could scrape together going at the village shop in powder, shot, and patches, the stock purchase being: one pound of shot 4d., three ounces of powder 6d., and sixteen patches 1½d. – total 11½d., which would provide sixteen shots, with the usual charge of 3 drachms powder to 1 ounce of shot.

Wads were a matter of but little difficulty, for we had our own wad-cutters, by means of which, together with heavy mallet and a block of wood, we could quickly punch out any number of wads from old cardboard boxes.

At times, however, so great was the demand, even old cardboard boxes were not forthcoming, whereon the exigencies of war demanded that we should unostentatiously remove any suitably covered book from its bookshelf, punch the cover full of holes, and promptly replace the volume: such practice not being favoured by our elders and betters.

The cleaning of muzzle-loaders is far from being the simple operation that breach-loaders call for, for which reason a gun would be used as long as possible before it was washed out, though an oiled rag would always be applied externally before replacing a weapon in its rack.

Also, the powder exploding in the bare barrel instead of within the card-board shell of a cartridge, caused much quicker fouling, so that after twenty or thirty shots had been fired, the gun would begin to kick badly, while often the brass head of the ramrod would be inclined to stick when ramming down a wad.

Our cleaning rods were made by the local carpenter of elm, such wood being fibrous and not liable to snap off inside the barrel.

Through a small hole in the end of the rod, a hank of tow would be inserted and then wound round and round the rod till of suitable thickness.

The barrel having been taken out of the stock, its breech end would be placed in a half-filled pail and left a few minutes so that water might soak in through the nipple, before the tow-tipped cleaning rod was inserted into the muzzle, and then worked up and down the whole length of the barrel.

This action was just like that of a pump, albeit there being no spout to carry off water sucked in through the nipple, a forceful downward thrust of the cleaning rod, besides creating a loud gurgling and screeching in the pail, would cause a jet of foul-smelling, ink-black liquid to squirt out of the muzzle, staining hands, arms, and anything else with which it came in contact.

Water that had been sucked into the barrel could be squirted out again through the nipple to a distance of twenty or thirty feet, and this was always done whenever any one came within range who could be used as a target.

Two or three changes of water were necessary before the barrel was thoroughly cleansed, and then two or three changes of tow before it was properly dried, after which a wipe out with oiled tow or rag put the finishing touch.

It was a long, dirty job, taking fully half an hour, and I would emerge from the struggle drenched, and black as a tinker, for my services were frequently in requisition at the price of one or two shots.

My brothers were often away shooting at different places in the neighbourhood, but for ordinary daily practice, sparrows flying about the premises afforded excellent sport; and on a windy day it was not so easy to bring down one of those hardy little birds on their quick, jerky flight.

We would all assemble in the turnip shed, keeping a sharp lookout for sparrows passing to and fro between a neighbouring farm and an old fir tree where they used to nest and roost in great numbers, and take shots in turn.

It was on one of these occasions that I made my first really successful shot, being at the time between six and seven years old.

Having earned a shot or two by dint of much hard work, I assembled in grandeur with the others, impatiently awaiting my turn, which was last.

A strong northerly wind brought the sparrows right overhead at a great height and pace.

Miss after miss was recorded, each followed by elaborate excuses and explanations, till finally the supreme moment arrived, when the short single-barrel, lightly charged, was handed to me with many condescending instructions.

Look out, here comes a sparrow!

Stepping to the front, trembling with excitement and eyes watering, I made out the dark, jerking speck coming straight towards me.

Raising the gun and aiming well in front, as father had so often advised, I pulled the trigger, and down came my bird like a stone, amidst general exclamations of amazement.

I had wiped the eyes of all the others, and so great was my joy, that their unanimous verdict of 'It was just by accident', left me quite untouched; and when father presently strolled up and said 'Well done! it was a capital shot', I felt at once both humble and speechless with overwhelming content.

On my ninth birthday father presented me with a new single-barrel muzzle-loader, sixteen bore, for my very own, to keep and use exactly as I liked; the only conditions imposed being that I was never to point it at any one, loaded or unloaded, and that I was never to shoot anything sitting, but give everything a fair chance.

It was a beauty! The barrel was bronzed in tiny brown rings, while the ramrod looked like ebony, with bright brass tips. Also, there was a leather shot bag, with shoulder strap complete, and a lovely bronze-looking powder-flask.

The very first day after its arrival, accompanied by my fox-terrier Marky, I bowled over a hare, a rabbit, and a peewit without a miss, in some fields adjoining the house.

It was a tremendous victory, and even nowadays I frequently think of it with feelings of deep satisfaction.

In any rider to hounds what hosts of memories are awakened by that grand old song:

> *'Tis a fine hunting day*
> *And as balmy as May,*
> *There's a fox in the spinney they say!*

With any gunner of my native swamp, what memories cluster round the magic words, 'Coot shootin'!'

Way back to earliest recollection, 'coot shootin' ' stood for highest pinnacle of the sportsman's desire.

Coots breed in great numbers amongst the dense reed-beds of all Norfolk Broads, but when the reeds are mostly cut, or stripped of their leaves by early frosts, these 'bold, adventurous' birds congregate in hundreds and sometimes thousands on the open waters of Hickling Broad, where the sponge-like weed, growing upwards to within a foot or two of the surface, provides them with an attractive and inexhaustible food supply.

Should severe cold set in and the Broad become frozen, the whole swarm will disappear in one night, to seek open water on tidal rivers and estuaries farther south, or to congregate on salt marshes by the sea, if not on the sea itself.

All through autumn the question of coots was constantly discussed. 'Were leaves off the reeds?' 'Not yit; there want another good frost or tu.' 'How many coots were there?' 'A good few, fare to be a matter er fower or five hund'ed' 'When was the coot shooting to be?' 'Doan' know; the Rarverand heant said norrin' as yit'.

Then intense anxiety would be felt lest a sudden severe

frost should lay the Broad and drive away all the coots before a day was fixed: 'They kaep a pourrin' orf an' a pourrin' orf till all the cutes 'll be gorne, see if they beant'.

Then suddenly the news would flash through the whole countryside: 'Cute shutin' a Monday'. 'Hooray!' and as no invitations were issued or expected in those days, every one who could, instantly made preparations to attend.

Breech-loaders were still few and far between, and generally spoken of as new-fangled, dangerous, and poor killers, for which reason every one borrowed for the occasion all the muzzle-loaders he could, so that, there being but little time for reloading when the coots began to rise, he might have ready to hand as large a battery as possible of loaded guns which he had only to pick up and fire.

The first coot shooting I attended officially was just after my ninth birthday and the arrival of my new gun, but as for months past I had been maturing plans, on the great day the fore part of my boat bristled with four weapons carefully laid out on an old rug.

Besides my own beautiful sixteen bore, I had borrowed from old Trickler a tiny, rusty single-barrel which had belonged to his son Harry, who, twenty years before, had 'gorne down to the Nowth'. From the local shopkeeper I had borrowed a twenty bore double-barrel converted flint-lock, but as the right-hand nipple had blown out, only the left-hand barrel could be used; while from the small farmer and local preacher, I had borrowed a cast-steel single-barrel, fourteen bore, which he had bought at an auction for five and sixpence; so that, all told, I mounted four guns, or rather, four barrels, each polished up, oiled, and loaded with extreme care; though as they were all of different bores, it was necessary to have four sizes in wads, four piles of which were accordingly placed on the rug, each by the corresponding weapon.

It had long been arranged that Jethro, who was about my own age, should shove me in Peter's little boat for the sum of eighteenpence.

On Monday morning the whole neighbourhood was astir, while by ten o'clock the Bank was lined with traps of various descriptions, sportsmen, mostly with a gun under each arm, walking up and down chatting and joking, and marshmen in blue guernseys, long crotch boots and sou'westers, waiting to shove the different boats, which, to the number of twenty or more, were lined up along the shore.

Jethro and I were first afloat, with guns, wads, powder, shot, and patches all carefully laid out on the old rug spread in the fore part, while I sat immediately behind on a board laid athwairt the gunnels, Jethro standing in the stern, quant in hand, all ready.

A flail basket contained our lunch of sausage rolls, bread and cheese, raw onions, and four bottles of ginger beer.

What were we waiting for? Should we never start? We were losing so much time!

At last there was a general stir, every one making for the boats, and then I caught sight of the Rarverand's commanding figure just leaving Old Tom's cottage, where he had apparently been quietly sitting till all was reported ready, when he gave the order to start.

Splendid! All the boats shoved up the deek a little way and then drew to either side so that the Rarverand, quanted by Old Tom, might pass.

He gave me a smiling nod, viewed my armament with

twinkling eyes, swung round on his seat and said something to Old Tom whereat they both shook with laughter,
and the fleet was away.

I felt a cold, sinking feeling internally, while Jethro
was so excited he accidently splashed two portly occupants
of the next boat, who angrily demanded why we boys were
not at home, to which Jethro replied wrathfully 'Hold
yow yer own', as he shoved our boat clear, and then
explained to me that 'them tu fules baent er no account':
the same being well-known auctioneers.

There was a strong northerly breeze, which, it was said,
would keep the coots from mounting very high.

Presently the boats began spreading out into an
extended, crescent formation, and, keeping about fifty
yards apart, swept on towards Eddy's Corner, where the
coots were known to be.

Every man or boy in the neighbourhood who could
find up anything in the shape of a gun, no matter how
antiquated, was either aboard one of the boats or had
taken up a post of vantage somewhere ashore, for which
reason the banks of the Broad were thickly lined with
anxiously waiting nimrods, so that our crescent having
extended and advanced its wings to either side of Eddy's
Corner, the poor coots were completely surrounded – by
guns in boats on one side, and by guns ashore on the
other.

Coots do not take wing easily, always running for some
distance along the surface, into the wind, before they can
rise clear of the water.

Presently some wildfowl rose, mounted to a great
height, and passed safely over the guns.

Next, a few isolated coots took wing, to be promptly

dropped on reaching the oncoming line of boats.

Then after a few minutes of intense excitement, during which our crescent crept slowly onwards, the great body of coots began to move, some running along the water this way, some that, and gradually rising into the air, till dozens, scores, hundreds of them were all simultaneously seeking to pass over the encirling guns.

Two or three advance shots to begin with, then a perfect roar, while dead birds struck the water in all directions.

I got my eye on to one, which was coming straight at me, about fifteen yards high, and was just going to pull the trigger, when 'bang' from the neighbouring boat, and down he came.

It was most disconcerting, but instantly seeing another one almost over me, I hurriedly took aim, fired, and missed! Awful disaster; but no time for regrets, as dozens were bearing down on us, like black bombshells.

Catching up the local preacher's weapon, I lowered a bird in style, though at the same moment was intensely surprised to hear a thin 'pip' just over my head, when turning for an instant, I realized that Jethro, forgetting every right principle in the excitement, had laid hands on old Trickler's little gun and also brought down his coot: two in the water at once and no time to bandy words.

The grocer's left-hand-barrel-converted then spoke, but without definite result, and I was reloading for dear life, with coots flying all round like gnats on a summer's evening.

Jethro picked up one of our birds, but the other was calmly appropriated by the auctioneers, who refused to give it up, thereby extracting the epithet 'hungry warmin' from my companion.

The uproar was not yet over, and I dropped another with my re-load, while a bird, wounded from some other boat, fell thump into the water not three feet off, splashing me from head to foot, and being lifted aboard by Jethro in the twinkling of an eye – which made three.

The firing line was now all in confusion, each boat being independently engaged in chasing cripples, despite Old Tom's stentorian roars of 'Kaep tegither, tegither', and which eventually brought forth an irritated rejoinder from someone of 'There's that bowtiful woice agin', provoking general laughter, and after which no further commands were issued.

Presently, however, the crescent was more or less reformed, and we made for Holcombe Pit and Stony Bank at the further end of the Broad, where many coots had settled, and there I added another to the bag: four.

Then we came all the way back to our starting-point, where the terrified coots had now collected, and here I secured two more: six.

Ashore, several of my village friends and acquaintances, lurking behind furze bushes along the Smea, did fairly well, while one little old character, rejoicing in the appetizing nickname of 'Game-pie', had climbed up Fenn's pump wind-mill, so as to be nearer any coots passing over.

One did pass over, and was promptly lowered, but the gun being evidently over charged, kicked so hard that Game-pie lost his foothold and came down a matter of fourteen feet or so with a run, head first, though luckily, landing in the sluice, he got off with nothing worse than a ducking.

My old playmate 'Slam', taking a holiday from coal

carrying, was also there with an ancient blunderbuss, but having no gun licence, he pretended to be cutting furze with a long handled wood-hook.

I saw a well-known sportsman in one of the boats nearest the shore miss an easy shot both barrels, but the coot edging landwards, was immediately doubled up by the blunderbuss.

At the same time I saw our new peeler pushing his way through furze and swamp towards Slam, to ask for his licence, but the gun having been quickly concealed in a drain, he was asked with withering scorn whether it were possible to shoot coots with a wood-hook.

This finished the first round, and we now had lunch aboard our boats lined up round the First War Bush, taking about half an hour, after which a start was made on round number two, when I accounted for another brace: eight.

Half way down the Broad it rained for a few minutes, whereon our auctioneer friends put their guns under the fore part of their punt, to keep dry, but in getting them out again, both barrels of one somehow went off, blowing a hole through the bottom of the boat, so that she sank with all on board in about five feet of ice-cold water, to the amusement of every one and the intense satisfaction of myself and Jethro, who gleefully remarked: 'Sarve 'em right. Tharrull larn 'em wit, I'll lay a guinea'.

The third and final round brought us but one addition to the bag, making nine, for there were hardly any coots left, all having been either killed or scared away.

Friend Geoffrey's was head boat, as usual, with twenty-five birds, for he was a magnificent shot, while the total number killed must have been between three and four hundred.

Wet, stiff with cold and smoke begrimed, I staggered home with guns and coots; hungry and tired out, but filled with the proud contentment of victory bravely won.

Monte Carlo and Cannes may have their fashionable pigeon shootings, but, if trap shooting there must be, give me a good old 'sparrer metch' such as were held in my native village on Shrove Tuesdays for a leg of pork put up by the Greyhound Inn.

For two or three days previous, Naylor the rat-catcher, and Game-pie would be out o' nights catching sparrows, the Dairy-house barn being an especially good place, till they had several dozens in sacks and covered baskets.

The trap would be set up in a ploughed field close by, and at about two o'clock in the afternoon shooting would commence in presence of a large and appreciative crowd.

The competitors were mostly hefty, thickset marshmen, with long single-barrel guns of large calibre, suitable for wild-fowling.

Into these weapons they would pour enormous charges of powder and shot, ladled out of little calico bags and measured with clay pipe-bowls.

The usual rules of trap shooting were observed: twenty-two or twenty-five yards rise, and the sparrow to fall within a fixed radius.

On account of its diminutive size, negative colouring and sprightly flight, a trapped sparrow is as hard to hit as a trapped pigeon; so that these contests were always keen, as well as productive of excellent marksmanship; the proud winner receiving in addition to the leg of pork a full meed of general admiration.

I am, however, dead against trap shooting of any kind,

as being a lazy, cruel, unfair, and therefore unsportsman-like pastime. A condition imposed when I received my first gun was 'give everything a fair chance', and so long as I am the man behind the gun, that condition still holds good, and a fair chance everything shall get.

Of other shooting – snipe, partridge, hare, pheasant – there is any amount in Norfolk, but such being of the ordinary, well-known kinds, it is unnecessary for me to dwell upon them.

CHAPTER VI

The Broads

A GRAVEL path three feet wide by thirty yards long, with a drop of two feet to the fore deck on one side and backed by a six-foot privet hedge on the other, led from the Pleasure Boat Inn to the front staithe: a wedge-shaped piece of greensward somewhat larger than a tennis court, projecting between the back and fore decks towards the open Broad, and fringed with willow trees sheltering a tumbledown, thatched shed.

It was a bright summer morning with hot sun and gusty westerly breeze.

Unusual bustle had replaced the ordinarily trance-like quietude of the Pleasure Boat Inn.

Without, three or four sedate-looking cobs, harnessed to high square carts and hitched to convenient gate posts, seemed almost to beat time with dull hoof thuds, in attempts to free their legs from the attentions of hungry flies.

Within, the sound of loud, cheery voices, bursts of laughter, and the frequent rattle of pint-pots on bare wooden tables, denoted brisk business.

But it was the narrow path leading to the front staithe that claimed every attention, for along its whole length lay boats of various sizes, shapes, colours, and ages, all lateen rigged, with sails hoisted and flapping in the breeze, while aboard or on the path, men and youths with rolled-up sleeves were putting the finishing touches: a new lashing here, a block changed there, a few stitches in the leech to prevent quivering, and throwing up water on to the sails to make them hold the wind.

It was Hickling water-frolic, and the first match was about to start.

Berthed nearest the Broad lay the Rarverand's *Thorn* with Old Tom, two of his sons, Grandson Albert, and big Dick Suggate, the boat-builder, aboard by way of crew.

It was the day of lateeners in those remote waters. Whence the peculiar model and picturesque rig came I do not know, but both have now long since disappeared, never to return.

The *Thorn*, winner of many a hard sailed race, embodied all the best points of this curious class.

Her actual hull was about fourteen feet long, though an enormous square eight-foot counter stern lying almost clear of the water, gave her a length over all of, say, twenty-two feet.

Half-decked, bows broad and bluff, and a nine-foot beam, she presented a very tubby appearance, though below water her lines were fine, with a two-foot iron keel and a large rudder swinging below the counter.

Painted, black sides with vermilion streak round gunnel, red bottom, and slate colour on decks and inside well, she looked very smart and impressive.

Her short, thick foremast, stepped right in the bows with a strong rake forrard, carried an enormous lateen sail with a yard about forty feet long, and an eighteen-foot boom swinging just clear of the mizzen-mast.

Almost burying herself in the water, throwing up a big bow-wave, and drawing a small mountain astern, that enormous sail-spread still forced her along at great speed, and she would roar majestically by with all the power and swell of a steam launch.

Beating into the wind was her strong point, for besides sailing very close, she went about like a flash, and without losing hardly any way; while running before a strong breeze was dangerous work, as her towering mainsail, pressing down on the foremast raking right over the bows, forced her farther and farther into the water, till she would crash along, bows level, with all hands congregated on the counter to keep her from running under.

In the first match were the *Thorn*; the *Maria*, another noted racer belonging to a sporting farmer; the *Ethel*, always down by the bows and up by the stern; the *B.B.* and several others, though the *Ethel's* enormous yard having snapped in two shortly after starting, the race soon resolved itself into a duel between the *Thorn* and the *Maria*, of which Old Tom, as usual, just managed to get the better.

All the neighbourhood for miles round seemed to be there, for the Broad was thickly dotted with wherries and boat-loads of sightseers being either sailed or quanted about so as to get good views of the racing.

Just before the second match, general attention was claimed by Harold, who, having borrowed a large lateen sail from Old Peyton, the innkeeper, had hoisted it on his little green boat, which, caught dead aft by a strong puff, flew out of the front deek at the rate of knots, sheering about and rolling so wildly from side to side as to alternately ship water over both gunnels, while Harold worked frantically at the helm to avoid ramming other craft, till finally she capsized to windward and sank in open water about a hundred yards out, amidst prolonged cheering.

On the staithe a troop of niggers provided music and much merriment, while the continuous roar of voices from the inn parlour proclaimed a busy day for the trade.

Sailing races over, excitement centred round a sculling match, which, after several false starts, numerous fouls, one fight, which carried both combatants overboard and was continued in five feet of water, and endless hard language, was won by Tom Goose of Horsey; while a quanting match was carried off by Old Tom's son Noll, who, in his prime, took a lot of beating.

Next day we learned that more fights than usual had kept matters lively at the Pleasure Boat till a late hour, and as several of the gladiators had been 'pulled', water-frolic interest continued unabated till fitting pains and penalties had been inflicted by the local magistrate.

Barton Broad, four miles from Hickling by road but more than twenty by river, was a fine sheet of water with good depth in those days, though latterly it has become much choked up by dense growths of weed.

Barton water-frolic was an important annual fixture at which most of the local cracks competed.

I remember driving over one morning with father and joining the Rarverand and Activity in a large flat-bottomed boat anchored amongst low reeds and in such a position as to command a good view of the whole Broad.

Both the *Thorn* and the *Maria* were sailing in the principal race, together with half a dozen other lateeners and one big white cutter, which, it being the first occasion such a rig had competed in those waters, gave rise to great comment and a good deal of apprehension amongst local owners.

It was a cloudy day and blowing so hard that most of

the boats would have reefed had it not been that an upset in those shallow waters spelt nothing worse than a ducking, for which reason every stitch of canvas was hoisted by all, on the sporting chance.

The race was four times up and down an S-shaped course, in all about seven miles; starting from fixed moorings and drawing lots for berths.

The *Thorn* had her usual crew aboard, and Old Tom, luckily drawing No. 1, got the windward lay.

How those boats roared through the water when manoeuvring to take up positions, heeling right over beneath their forty-foot spars till even keels could sometimes be seen! It was most exciting, but suddenly they were all in a beautiful line, with snow-white sails fluttering and cracking like whips in the gale, when 'bang' went the starting gun, and they were off.

At the report the old *Thorn* seemed to shoot right ahead, gaining a lead of perhaps forty yards within the first half minute, and there she stuck for the whole race, with the other eight boats hard on her heels like a pack of hounds, leaving behind them lanes of foam, and sending up a combined roar that carried to the furthest limits of the Broad.

You never saw such a sight! The poor old *Thorn* looked just like a hunted deer, settling down into the water as though straining every nerve to escape, while each minute our hearts were in our mouths as she staggered wildly beneath her towering cloud of canvas: 'She can't live'. 'Yes, she can'. 'Ah-h-h!' as she gibed round the top buoy and half her foresail was in the water, followed by an involuntary cheer as she gathered herself together again.

Once there seemed no hope, the Rarverand exclaiming

'She's gone!' and lowering his field glasses; but lo! with sails almost flat on the water, and all her crew perched on the windward side, she luffed and slowly righted, and then tore on past us like a train, her bows smothered in foam, big Suggate standing right aft, Albert frantically working at the pump, and Old Tom with set face and hand on the tiller, watching her every move, while the swell she rolled broke over and almost swamped our boat.

The *Maria* and the big white cutter were the worst, for first one and then the other would draw right up, till we thought the *Thorn* must be caught, and then die away again, but only apparently to gather up strength for a fresh attack.

During the last round the wind, if anything, increased, and several boats came to grief, though every one was too absorbed in the deadly struggle between the three leaders to pay heed to aught else.

At last the gun fired, as our good old *Thorn* twenty yards ahead of the cutter, fled past the winning flag, to be instantly shot up into the wind by Old Tom: the strain over, the race won! Hip, hip, Hooray!!

The Rarverand always stammered a little, and now, albeit making plenty of noise, was perfectly inarticulate; though a decanterful of his excellent sherry was soon in circulation, while his beaming, jovial face told its own tale.

Presently Old Tom, alternately mobbing and laughing from sheer excitement, brought the *Thorn* under bare poles slowly alongside, when every incident of the race was retailed for the Rarverand's benefit.

Then Activity unpacked the well stocked luncheon-basket, and handed round great platefuls of cold game-pie, chicken and ham, beef patties, salad, jam puffs, bread and cheese and celery; all of which disappeared before inundations of Allsop's bottled ale.

In the very midst, a committee man brought alongside the *Thorn*'s prize – six beautiful silver salt-cellars and spoons in a silk-lined leather case – and everything was perfect.

Although the cutter did not win, she had given local champions a taste of her quality, and that memorable race sounded the knell of the picturesque but somewhat dangerous and cumbersome lateen rig, for cutters were soon in general vogue, and I do not remember a lateener ever again winning a race.

The enormous length of the mainsail yard rendered it liable to snap, as well as placing the leverage of its very considerable weight together with accompanying sail pressure, at a great height above the boat, and the foremast being stepped right in the bows with a strong rake forrard, there was a dangerous tendency to run underwater.

Strange to say, lateeners which I have seen in the Red Sea, all had their foremasts stepped much further back *with a strong rake aft*, and instead of lowering yards in order to furl sails, booms were hauled up to the yards, while in strong winds and heavy seas, there was not the least tendency to run under, in fact, quite the reverse.

Two or three days after the water-frolic I again found myself, uninvited, aboard the *Thorn*, in company with the Rarverand and her usual crew, including Activity in charge of the lunch-basket and two gallons of six-ale in a big stone bottle.

With two reefs in the huge racing mainsail and the cup flag flying proudly at our peak, we bowled across Barton

Broad on the twenty-mile sail through beautiful winding rivers, back to Hickling.

Over Irstead Shoals, with thatched cottages and a dear little church by the water, in a setting of fine old English oaks; by Howe Hill, boasting a lofty windmill and an extremely deep well on its summit; passing, with lowered masts and sails, under quaint old Ludham Bridge; and then laying to at ruined St Benet's Abbey for lunch.

The day was fine, the breeze was fair, our cup flag proclaimed the *Thorn* winner to all passing craft, and we aboard felt good and well.

The stone bottle had not been forgotten, though little flaky specks floating in the beer drew from Old Tom the remark that 'hops must be cheap ter year', which passed as handsome wit, provoking general laughter.

An excellent luncheon, a stroll amongst the ruins, another glass of beer with hops, and we were off again.

Shooting by Thurne Mouth, where masses of dark green bull-rushes fringed the broad and tidal stream, we reached Heigham Bridge at about three o'clock, when it began to drizzle, with wind falling light and five miles still to go, though frequent pulls at the stone bottle kept our crew in high spirits, despite the ever present flaky specks.

Through Candle Deek, Narroways, over the Sounds and Whittlesea, we reached Deep Deek by five o'clock, and could just see Hickling Broad opening out through the now heavy rain, when darting from amongst the reeds, a flat-bottomed boat drew alongside, the dripping occupant, a thin, tallish man with a long beard, holding on to the *Thorn*'s gunnel and showering on the Rarverand a torrent of congratulations.

It was John Crapes, thatcher, marshman, wildfowler and fisherman.

When at last the Rarverand could get a word in, it was to ask if Mr Crapes could drink a glass of beer.

Mr Crapes could, certainly he could, though of course he had thought of no such thing when coming alongside.

Activity looked deeply concerned, holding the enormous bottle to his ear with both hands and shigging it vigorously, while Old Tom thought there might be 'just one more glass if yer squeeze her right tight'.

Crapes held forth a tumbler, over which Activity turned the bottle upside down, when out shot some dregs of beer together with the mouldering skeleton of a mouse: strong even in death, and origin of those flaky hops!

Fishing out and holding up the delinquent by its tail, Crapes looked thirstily from the half-tumblerful of dregs to the faces of that horror-stricken crew, and then letting go the gunnel, shoved back into the reeds, talking as he went.

As for the crew, they trembled and quaked and brought forth laughter mingled with tears, oblations to that ridiculous mouse.

Wherries are peculiar to the Norfolk Broads.

I do not mean neat little rowing boats such as are called wherries on the Thames, but long, low-lying barges of twenty tons and upwards, with raised hatches amidships, foot-wide plankways on either side, and carrying one enormous sail.

The mast, weighted at its foot with about a ton and a quarter of lead, stands well forrard in a tabernacle, and, working on a pivot just clear of the hatches, it balances exactly, like a see-saw, and so can be quickly lowered or raised with the greatest of ease.

The sail, of thickest canvas, dressed with a mixture of herring oil and tar till it is jet black, very heavy, and almost as stiff as a board, has a gaff but no boom, and is hoisted with a single halliard by means of a winch and crank.

A man and a boy generally make up the crew, but sometimes a man and his wife; who have a nice little cabin aft, opening from a well, standing in which a single hand can work the tiller and at the same time tend the sheet, for while one of the two massive quadruple blocks is attached to the toe of the sail, the other works to and fro on an iron horse across the cabin roof, so that the sheet comes well to hand, when a couple of turns round a cleat holds all taut.

The hull is always dressed with tar, the hatches are painted red, a white band runs round the gunnel and a white shield tips the bow; the hatch panels and tabernacle stanchions are frequently picked out in dark blue, while a large, red vane adorns the masthead, the general effect being workmanlike and quaintly picturesque, reminiscent of Dutch luggers.

Deep loaded, a wherry only draws about four feet, and light, perhaps two feet less.

Their sailing qualities are excellent: fast, handy, safe; and with huge, board-like sails hauled right flat, they will draw along almost into the wind's eye.

When breezes are light or dead ahead, one hand in the well will attend to tiller and sheet, while the other will help her along by using an enormous quant, iron-shod at one end and capped with a flat, circular shoulder-button at the other.

Standing on the fore-peak and getting a firm set to leeward with the iron-sheathed toe, he will place the button against his shoulder, and then leaning far forward and pushing with all his might, will walk, almost on all fours, along the plank-way right aft, before withdrawing the quant with a jerk and going forward again to get another set.

Nowadays, many of these traders are converted into 'pleasure-wherries' during the summer months, the hatches being raised, windows let in, the hold panelled and divided off into spacious cabins, tables, crockery, beds and other requisites provided, until they are capable of taking parties of six or seven, and are by far the most comfortable yachts in which to make a two or three weeks' cruise on the Norfolk Broads.

At most water-frolics there was a match for wherries, sometimes to start with masts and sails lowered, it being a matter for great excitement as to which would get her towering black sail fully hoisted first; and five or six of those graceful craft 'snoring' along in half a gale made a striking picture.

A wave of patriotic excitement passed over the whole of Broadland when it became known that the then Prince of Wales, our late revered King, was to visit the neighbouring town of Great Yarmouth, and every one who could, instantly made preparations to attend.

We had no railway in those days, so that the distance of sixteen miles was still a very considerable one. Most drove, a good few walked.

Harold had arranged to go by sea with the coastguards from Palling, but, being a very careful dresser, he spent so long in adjusting his collar, that the boat was already half a mile distant when he reached the beach, so he gave chase along the sands, and after keeping it up for about five miles, the good-natured tars lowered sail, put ashore, and took him aboard, hot, tired, and his collar all adrift.

As for myself, I took a free passage for the round trip aboard the corn-laden wherry *Emily* of our port, owned by Mr George Deals, son of Old George of that ilk, whose son and grandson, George, went as skipper, while his younger brother, Slam, nine years old like myself and one of my village friends, filled the position of first mate.

Mr Deals had hired land of father for a quarter of a century on a verbal agreement, and paid rent when he liked, which was always when it was due, if not before; a lease for the land and receipts for the rent being considered quite unnecessary as between man and man.

Mr Deals's house had been struck by lightning. He kept a cow, a sow, a donkey, a horse named 'Boxer', and besides the land, did a nice little business in coals and pig foods by means of the wherry.

Therefore, I embarked early one morning with reliable friends, while a strong breeze from the most favourable quarter, nor'west by north, promised a quick passage.

Running free, we soon covered the five miles to Heigham Bridge, on approaching which Slam dived down into the fore-peak to free the foot of the mast from its retaining clamps, and when within a hundred yards of the massive old-time structure, rapidly lowered the sail; and then, just as we shot under the low, stone arch, our enormous mast swung gracefully down till it lay flat upon the hatches; to as gracefully swing up again the moment we were through, and be instantly clamped below, as well as made fast to the bows by a thick wire fore-stay, after which we both set to work cranking up the sail with all our might, so that the *Emily* gathered way again and continued her voyage without making any stop.

We had a fair wind practically the whole way, necessitating several gibes, when the huge sail and heavy sheets swung over with such terrific crashes that it seemed to me as if either the iron horse or the top of the cabin must be torn bodily away.

The *Emily* also glided under Acle Bridge without bringing to, while at Stokesby Ferry we caught the ebb-tide, which put us into Yarmouth in time for supper, consisting of red herrings cooked over the cabin fire, bread and butter, Dutch cheese, mild ale and hot coffee; and then, having closed both door and port-holes to keep out the damp, we slept splendidly after our long day in the open air — the skipper on one bunk, myself on another, and Slam on the floor — in an atmosphere redolent of toasted cheese, herrings, beer, and coffee.

Next day the crew were hard at work discharging cargo, while I pursued Royalty from pillar to post, though mostly without success, owing to the dense crowd surging round and overtopping me each time the Royal carriage passed, till I could see little beyond the coat-tails of the man next in front.

Once, however, I saw the Prince well, at the moment when an old lady leaned far out from her carriage window and touched his uniform as he rode by, whereon His Royal Highness turned in the saddle, bowed and smiled, to the old lady's perfect delight.

In the evening there was a grand display of fireworks along the sea front, which so interested me that I advanced up the jetty to where rockets and coloured bombs were being let off, to be immediately chased by a policeman.

The display over, and carrying in triumph a sheaf of spent rocket sticks retrieved from the sands, I regained our yacht for the night.

On the morrow fortune was still against me till about seven in the evening, when, having just finished an ample tea at a pastrycook's, the Prince unexpectedly passed, whereon every one in the shop, customers and waitresses, all rushed out pell-mell.

Caught by the crowd, I was borne along in the wake of the royal carriage, but without catching a glimpse of its occupant, guiltily conscious the while that I had not paid for my tea.

As I could not return against that human flood, and as I heard people saying His Royal Highness was going to the theatre, to the theatre I went, paying a shilling for a second-row seat amongst the gods, and sitting with eyes glued to a vacant, crimson-covered chair in the stalls till about ten o'clock, when amidst general commotion and the 'National Anthem,' the chair was filled, and I gazed at the top of the Prince's head till midnight, when all was over, and I sought the pastrycook's to pay for my tea, only, however, to find the street deserted and the shop closed; so that, feeling an irredeemable criminal, I made for the wharf, spending my last shilling (the 'tea' shilling) at a stall on three boiled crabs, to enjoy with my messmates by way of a late supper.

With a full cargo of coals and maize, the voyage home against light head-winds took us nearly three days, but finally the *Emily* was safely berthed in the back deek.

The sail was still standing, and the skipper being busy

in the cabin rounding up, Slam and I took upon ourselves to lower it without orders.

I was at the winch slowly unwinding, while he clung on to the halliards to ease the strain, which caused my crank to suddenly slip off, with the result that Slam was jerked ten feet up the mast before he could let go, as the enormous sail came down with a crash, snapping the gaff into three pieces and bursting half the cogs off the winch.

It was all done in a moment, and who would have thought it!

I noted our skipper's pale face at the cabin door gazing on the wreckage with staring eyes, I observed Mr Deals, senior, slowly approaching up the lane, and I remember Slam and myself quietly but promptly quitting the scene for our respective homes.

It was late spring, and Old Tom had been doing up his boats, applying boiling tar below the water-line, inside and out (the Rarverand always referred to tar as 'Rudd's paint'), and putting on slate-coloured paint everywhere else.

I had spent a thoroughly enjoyable afternoon in the warm sun and yellow, blinding tar smoke, watching operations, proffering invaluable advice and lending a helping hand when not required.

Old Tom blazed away at Grandson Albert all the time 'fule' and 'wudden' being his usual terms of address, though for some inexplicable reason he tolerated me in silence.

I had been holding forth to Albert as to what kind of a boat I should buy so soon as funds would allow, when Old Tom completely staggered me by exclaiming: 'Yow'd berrer buy my little punt, she's for sale;' and then, seeing my look of stupefaction, went on to explain how his rheumatiz being that bad, he found the little punt too copply, and had told Dick Suggate to build him a right steady one for a matter of six pound ten, for which reason the little punt, done up right frayshe, tegither with quant, oars, sprit-s'l, bottom boards, and a place in the boat-house, could be mine for two pounds.

I travelled home at top speed, and for the next few days was supplementing my slender hoard of ready cash by the feverish sale of chickens, ducks, rabbits, ferrets, and any other realizable possession, till late on Saturday night I rushed into Old Tom's cottage, too breathless to speak, and put down two pounds on the table; and the little punt was mine.

The little punt was mine! I could hardly believe it!

On leaving Old Tom's, instead of returning straight home, I tiptoed to the boat-house, and groping my way in the dark, slipped aboard my yacht, and stayed quietly there for nearly an hour, feeling the decks, the sides, the seats, the sculls, the quant, the mast and sail, and, chief glory of all, the massive oak beam on which the big swivel had so often been mounted, and which bestowed a man-o'-war-like dignity on my first command.

Being the youngest of several boys who all spent much of their time on the water, I picked up sailing instinctively, like swimming and shooting, so that long before I owned the little punt at ten years old, the art of sailing seemed as simple to me as the art of walking; in fact, I cannot remember when I did not understand sailing. It had always formed part and parcel of my daily life, and there was no question about understanding or not understanding. Sailing existed, and it never occurred to me that there might have been no sailing.

For a few weeks everything was perfect, the sprit-sail, a square patch of calico six feet by eight with one side lashed to a short mast, and peaked by means of a ten-foot stick or 'sprit', being very easily hoisted, as well as lowered, rolled up round the mast, and stowed away in the fore-peak, while a scull out astern took the place of a rudder for steering, and which, together with six inches of keel forrard tapering off to nothing amidships, enabled me to haul a middling close wind.

The *Needle*, for such I christened her, was about eighteen feet long by four feet beam, with the sharp, wedge-shaped fore-part covered in for a length of seven feet. Then amidships came the well, eight feet long by sixteen inches deep and having side decks, while the pointed stern was also covered in for about three feet, so that she was very much like a large canoe, only far heavier and infinitely stronger, having been built of stout oak purposely to withstand the recoil of Old Tom's big swivel.

The season for shooting and rabbiting being over, both gun and ferrets were out of commission, so that during the whole of that summer, my attention was exclusively centred on sailing, and if I now had to say which I consider to have been the happiest time of my life, I think the verdict would be for those golden days of my first command.

Fine weather or foul, calm or gale, I was always on the Broad, brimming over with pride at each newly discovered quality of my tight little craft.

Accompanied by a little cripple friend, grandson of the village carrier, and seated on a cushion in the bottom of the well with my back resting against the after-deck, one hand holding the sheet and the other steering with a scull, we would skim lightly across the sunlit Broad, through narrow cuttings gay with white and yellow water-lilies and partly overgrown with tall, graceful reeds, till we shot out into Old Meadow Deek, a narrow river winding between banks bright with wild flowers and feathery reeds, backed by clumps of sallows and the towering sails of distant windmills.

Gliding on in perfect peace, shoals of dusky perch and pink-finned roach could be seen darting between stately lily stems down in the clear cool stream, water-hens would scuttle close across our bows, herons and snipe would lazily take wing from marshes on either side to settle down again a little farther off, while on reaching Horsey Mere, scores of startled coots would run along the water with a great pattering and splashing of feet, rise a yard or so into the air, and then in full flight, pitch down into safety near the edge of the reeds, cleaving the water with their breasts, and throwing off sparkling jets to either side.

Sailing on, wildfowl and sea-gulls would take wing, while the cadenced murmur of breakers could be heard from beyond that long line of dunes, which, a mile away, alternately shone white with sand and green with marram grass in the brilliant sunshine.

Returning to Meadow Deek and tying up to the bank, we would fish awhile and make tea, and then, the wind having completely died away, would scull slowly home in the sweet, restful calm of a Broadland eventide.

After a time, unalloyed success began to pall, and I became ambitious of making several additions and improvements to the *Needle*.

The first thing, of course, was to get greater speed, which necessitated a larger sail, and consequently a longer mast, as well as a gaff, a boom, and a new sheet with two single blocks.

Acting under Old Tom's advice, I bought fourteen yards of calico at sixpence a yard, out of which he very kindly cut me a 'leg-o'-mutton' mainsail, while his daughter-in-law Harriet stitched it for half a crown: total for sail, nine and sixpence.

Also, Old Tom had an enormous open-air boiler in which he tanned his nets, and as tan prevents mildew, I spent one whole glorious day in tanning my sail, albeit lowness of funds necessitated a stinting of ingredients with the result that instead of coming out a beautiful deep red, my mainsail for ever after held a light, blotchy, bad-egg colour: total for coals, pitch, oak-bark, etc., one shilling.

A rough fir pole, such as are used for scaffolding, cost me a shilling, and this was trimmed up and made into a beautiful fifteen-foot mast by Ben the carpenter for two and six, who at the same time cut a ten-foot gaff and an eleven-foot boom out of light material, for one and sixpence each: total for spars, six and sixpence.

A sixpenny linen line from the village shop, together with two small single blocks presented by Old Tom, provided new sheets; a similar line furnished halliards, brail, strop, and tack, with something to spare; while an eightpenny ferret line was long enough for both gaff and boom lashings: total for rope, one and eightpence; making a grand total of eighteen and eightpence – a heavy drain on the exchequer.

The result of this change of rig at such heavy cost was most disappointing.

A sailing boat, whatever her size, is really a complicated machine, the different parts of which react on each other in such a way that having once been brought into harmony, any radical change in one of them will upset the balance of the whole.

I had increased my sail area only, and the *Needle* was at once perfectly unmanageable in anything like a breeze.

The new sail reached six feet farther aft than did the old one, which so pressed her stern to leeward, while her bows were still held up by the six inches of keel forrard, that steering with an oar became hard work in a light breeze and altogether impossible in a blow.

Matters could not be allowed to remain in this unsatisfactory state, so as soon as I had collected sufficient funds, the *Needle* was again hauled out and six inches of keel put on for her whole length, while a rudder with yoke and lines was also added, at a total cost of eight and sixpence.

Even then she carried too much helm, often bringing right up into the wind, so that I got Old Tom to cut out a jib from four yards of calico, which, together with stitching and tanning, cost three and six.

This time I made the tan too strong, resulting in an almost black jib, which showed up in striking contrast with the light, blotchy mainsail.

This addition not only brought almost perfect balance, but also a great increase in speed, though the days of comfort on a cushion at the bottom of the boat were gone, for my sail area was now so large that I had always to sit perched up on the windward side, with main-sheet, jib-sheet, and rudder-line always in hand, much like driving, easing off and luffing at every puff; while even then she continually shipped water over the low gunnels, so that a few weeks later I had them raised from four to thirteen inches by placing half-inch planking all round, at a cost of eleven shillings, which gave me an almost perfect little craft for a total sum of four pounds one and eightpence.

A strip of cocoa-matting together with one or two cushions, carried off from the house, put the finishing touch.

Hardly a day passed but what I was out sailing, visiting every hole and corner of the Broad, making for and pitting the *Needle* against every sailing-boat that appeared, keeping an eye on coots, swans, wildfowl, and strangers, which last, should they happen to be anglers, at once assumed in local eyes almost the status of criminals, to worry and annoy whom in every possible way in hopes of driving them off, was held to be highly praiseworthy, if not almost a duty.

For this particular work the *Needle* was perfect.

Sometimes I would take one or two friends for a bathe.

At the corner of the Second War Bush, close to the Smea, there was a nice place about four feet deep with clean, sandy bottom; and that was our favourite resort.

One breezy summer's evening Slam, the little cripple 'Man', Marky and myself embarked in high spirits, and after a pleasant run round the Broad, chasing a loon and irritating some anglers, brought to at Sandy Bottom, cast anchor, lowered sails, and stripped for the bath.

Marky was whining and shivering as usual in most uncomfortable fashion, but as it was his 'way', we paid but little heed.

Being ready first, I took a header from the fore-peak,

and while still under water heard splunge, splunge, splash, as my comrades followed suit.

The water was delightful, and after a long dive, I had just got footing on the smooth sand, when hot, searing irons seemed to be drawn across my bare shoulders, to be immediately followed by Marky's little cold nose against my cheek. Despite the whining and shivering, he had followed his master overboard like a sportsman, and albeit sharp claws had cut long red lines across my back, I felt both pleased and proud as I swam with him back to the *Needle* and pushed him on board again.

This manoeuvre was repeated two or three times, till after much scolding, he seemed to realize that his proper place was in the boat and not in the water, and having ceased from worrying, we thought no more of him till we had finished our swim, when, getting back on board, we found him, dripping wet, curled up on top of our clothes.

My pleasure and pride diminished, while the others were distinctly sour, it not being their dog.

Man's clothes were not so thoroughly soaked as ours, for which reason he was dressed first, and then began hoisting the mainsail, which flapped and swung about in the strong evening breeze.

This he should not have done till we all were ready, but being wet and cold, was anxious to get home, and so disregarded Slam's angry protest: 'Wharriyer keep on messin' about w' that there sail for? Yow'll h' me overboard dreckly, see 'f yer don't.'

Slam was a true prophet! He had got on his socks, boots, and overalls, and was just struggling hard to force head and arms through a wet, tight-fitting shirt, when 'whack' came the boom across his chest, making him stagger and drawing through the shirt a frantic, muffled: 'Wharriyerkeeponmess', – when 'whack' again from the boom, and over he went backwards.

How he got out of the shirt, and how he got out of the water, I do not know, and for all the help Man or I could give him he might have been drowned half a dozen times, seeing that we were both helpless and speechless from laughter.

Not so Slam, for once back on board, till well landed at the boat-house, he told us repeatedly and exactly what he thought of us, of the boat, and of the dawg.

The terrible responsibility resting on captains of vessels is seldom realized by ordinary people.

When I eventually did go to school at the age of fourteen, I felt very much like a fish out of water, cricket, football, tennis, and racquets all being new to me, while in lessons my lot was with youngsters barely coming shoulder high; all of which was very distressing, besides leading at first to some attempts at patronage by boys as well as masters, though thanks to extensive reading on all kinds of subjects, and to the wild, outdoor life I had hitherto led, both as regards general information and ability to take my own part, I was soon treated with something not unlike respect.

Our housemaster, who, besides being fat, wearing a beard and bowling underhand daisy-cutters, was considered a disciplinarian; in which capacity he doubtless thought a little sitting on would do me good.

Perhaps it did, and perhaps I felt grateful; anyhow, I invited him to come on a few days' cruise during the summer holidays; and he came – in bowler hat, tail-coat, side-spring boots, and with night-shirt and a change wrapped up in brown paper. Tally-ho!

It was a fine but sultry morning when we weighed anchor and romped away before a hot, westerly breeze, with all sail set, was just about as much as the *Needle* could do with.

Somehow the disciplinarian seemed quite out of place in a boat, and shorn of all superiority, for besides admitting that he knew nothing of sailing, hoped, as he could not swim, that it was quite safe.

Of course it was quite safe, for I now was in command; but the end was not yet.

At Heigham Bridge everything had to be taken down and rehoisted, the intricacies of which procedure greatly impressed my passenger, more especially as on smartly lowering the mast over my shoulder, it struck something hard a resounding crack, when on looking round, I saw the bowler all caved in and the wearer in a crouching attitude with one arm raised as if to ward off a blow, while he explained with watering eyes that it did not matter: the which was a good thing.

An hour later we lay to for lunch, but had hardly commenced when a heavy thunderstorm which had been brewing up all morning broke with torrents of rain, so that having quickly lowered the mainsail, we crept under it in hopes of keeping dry.

I was all right in an old oiler, but my guest got pretty well soaked.

It cleared somewhat towards three o'clock and we were glad to start again.

After Thurne Mouth it was dead head-wind, and as the tide was also against us, we could make no headway either by tacking or sculling, so having handed the rudder lines to the disciplinarian, I jumped ashore with the tracking line.

Within five minutes the *Needle* had charged the bank twice, and then suddenly sheered straight out into midstream, till I had to let go the tow-rope to avoid being pulled in.

There she lay in the middle of the river, broad side on, and being borne quickly back again before wind and tide, with her excited passenger vainly jerking the rudder from side to side, messing about with one scull, and generally looking and proving to be absolutely futile. Also, it began to pour again.

I never felt more like 'I told you so' in all my life!

Luckily or unluckily, the elements and a friendly bend brought the derelict within reach, so that having regained my tracking line, I was just about to make a fresh start, when, without warning, the master jumped for the shore, missing it by a trifle and going in well above both knees.

Crawling out of the mud, he declared that nothing should induce him to go back into the boat alone, while being soaked to the skin and numb with cold, he would positively like to do the tracking.

Nothing could be better. Steering comfortably on the back seat, I grinned to myself at sight of the bowler, the black tail coat shining with wet, and the side-spring boots ploughing along the sodden bank between walls of lofty rushes, which, swept by the tracking line, showered down cataracts of water upon the toiling slave.

This lasted the whole afternoon, till having passed under Ludham Bridge, we resolved to pitch camp for the night beneath a clump of willows on the river bank.

Having first lighted the paraffin stove and put the

kettle on, I drew a loose lashing round the scull handles, and then planting the blades well apart in the grass, so formed cross-trees on which to rest the thin end of the mast, when, throwing the mainsail over the framework thus formed, we had a serviceable tent in less than five minutes, into which we carted all our belongings, mostly wringing wet, though, fortunately, not the brown paper parcel, so that a change into dry clothes wrought a vast improvement both in the appearance and comfort of my ship-mate.

Hot tea, hot soup, hot eggs, bread and butter, a large cold apple-tart with milk and sugar, and some fresh strawberries, cheered us both up, and after he had lighted a pipe, I really believe the disciplinarian began to pridefully look upon himself as a wild, lawless, desperate sort of a buccaneer; and when at dusk two shots suddenly rang out quite close to the tent, flaring their red tongues, he may well have imagined a night attack by Indians, though on an old marshman presently quanting up with a brace of fine mallard by way of casualties, an indemnity of two shillings each procured for us the spoils of war.

Having spread out in the tent two or three damp wraps and covered them with the jib, we turned in early, being very tired after our long strenuous day; and no reference being made to the night-shirt, we simply took off boots and lay down in our clothes.

I was soon asleep, and should have passed an excellent night but for consciousness of continual moaning and restlessness on the part of my companion, who towards midnight gave me a real scare by jumping up with a kind of a screech and dashing out of the tent.

He explained afterwards that having placed the bowler

over his face to keep off the damp, he had just fallen asleep, when a large moth found its way inside the hat and set up a most awful fluttering and buzzing right on his face, which gave him such a turn, that, forgetting where he was, he had instinctively jumped up and dashed outside.

I noted regretfully that if he had only gone another yard he would have been in the river, and then got off to sleep again.

In the morning he looked a wreck, the result of practically no sleep, besides having rheumatism in the shoulder and a stiff neck from lying on the damp ground.

A good hot breakfast and a pipe made him feel better even to naming the site of our camp 'Point Jolly', and when brilliant sunshine had driven away those white, pall-like marsh vapours, he was almost himself again, though towards noon, while I was navigating the *Needle* across Barton Broad, he slept the sleep of exhaustion at the bottom of the boat.

That afternoon we made Stalham in order to purchase a few stores, but no sooner had we landed than he declared letters might be awaiting him at the post office, and turning a deaf ear to my expressed intention of showing him the way, hurried off alone, returning almost immediately to say that, unfortunately, he had found a telegram calling him home at once.

I was somewhat taken aback, having made preparations for a full week's outing, but he was absolutely decided, and within half an hour I saw the brace of mallard, the bowler, coat-tails, brown paper parcel, and now widely yawning side-springs, mount the local carrier's cart and be driven off in the direction of Norwich.

He did not offer to show the telegram, while an unmistakable look of relief when safely in the cart somehow made me think of 'Sanctuary', so despite his profuse thanks, I could not but help feeling that the bird had escaped from out the hand of the fowler.

At school I made friends with a senior boy named York, who also came to stay with me during the holidays, when we made various trips together in the *Needle*, which so aroused his enthusiasm for sailing that on presently attaining man's estate and going up to Cambridge, he agreed to buy a fine little half-decked boat, balanced lug, which happened to be for sale, if I would provide a boathouse, look after her, and defray yearly upkeep, which I gladly consented to do, seeing that age was beginning to tell heavily on the poor old *Needle*; in which manner she passed as a handsome present into the hands of Jethro.

Our trips in the *Zephyr* all over Broadland were too numerous to relate in detail, but Yarmouth, Lowestoft, Beccles, Norwich and Wroxham we visited again and again, meeting with many kinds of adventure by the way.

On another occasion we had been sailing all day, having come about forty miles, and were so tired out on arriving at Burgh St Peters on the Waveney, that we just made the *Zephyr* fast to a wharf by bow and stern and turned in, lying, as usual, on blankets at the bottom of the boat with our heads towards the bows.

How long we had been asleep I do not know, when suddenly we were both standing on our heads, smothered in blankets, and punching each other hard, apparently in self-defence.

Eventually crawling out over the stern, we realized that, the tide having fallen about three feet, the *Zephyr* had been left suspended in mid-air secured by bow and stern to the wharf, till the bow-rope parting while the stern-rope held fast, she had fallen with a crash to an angle of forty-five degrees, which accounted for our unpleasant awakening.

Having noted that another half-inch would have let water over the gunnel, when we must have sunk, and having slacked off the stern-rope to get her once more on an even keel, we turned in again to finish the night.

Brysdale coxed the 'Varsity Eight Pitman's first year, when, breaking a long series of Oxford wins, they steered and stroked Cambridge to victory.

Following the race aboard the Cambridge steamer, I witnessed that triumph, though at cost of a new fawn-coloured suit, ruined by rain and smuts from the vessel's smoke-stack.

Brysdale and I were at the same college, and struck up a friendship which still firmly stands the test of years.

During the long vacation, we two sailed aboard the *Zephyr* on the best cruise I ever took part in, visiting practically all the Broads.

Starting on a Friday, we began badly, for when no further than Heigham Sounds, a perfect deluge fell quite unexpectedly from an almost clear sky.

To run the *Zephyr* into a thick reed-bush, drop sail, and spread a heavy tarpaulin over all, took less than a minute, though by that time everything, including ourselves, was pretty well drenched.

In a quarter of an hour the rain was over, and we got under way again, drying things as we sailed.

That night we slept at Thurne Mouth, and the following afternoon made Great Yarmouth, tying up amongst dozens of wherries in the North river, an unsavoury, heathenish place, so that we determined to take the early morning's flood over Breydon and reach more civilized surroundings for our Sunday rest.

By seven o'clock the flood was putting up strong in the North river, and as a stiff westerly breeze was blowing, before starting we took in all reefs and lashed the tarpaulin over the fore part of the well, in case of shipping seas, leaving just enough room aft for us to work the boat in.

Once out on Breydon, which is a salt-water estuary seven miles long, we were much surprised to find the ebb still running there like a sluice, so that until slack water, we had to beat against both wind and tide.

I never saw the *Zephyr* sail or handle better. She seemed to comprehend the task ahead and nerve herself for the struggle.

Cutting through the water like a steam launch, till our faces streamed down with driven spray, she raced backwards and forwards across that broad, windswept channel flowing swiftly between banks of slime and mud towards the open sea, sometimes gaining a few yards, though oftentimes barely holding her own.

Every minute we expected the tide to slacken, but it must have been a good two hours before there was any perceptible change, by which time we may have made perhaps half a mile.

It was desperately hard work, that constant tacking in the teeth of half a gale, but we now began to forge quickly ahead, though a heavy swell got up as soon as flood and wind met, and when the rising tide had just covered those slimy banks, it was difficult judging when to go about, with the result that once or twice we were within an ace of getting badly on the putty.

Far away across that desolate waste of mud-flats was a tiny speck, the Berney Arms Inn, standing in lonesome dreariness on a marsh at the top of Breydon; but on that Sunday morning what a beacon of hope it was!

We kept on saying: 'When we get to the Berney Arms' we would rest, have breakfast, lunch, get hot coffee. It was our longed-for haven.

Well, we got there at about one o'clock, thoroughly exhausted, wet, cramped, and faint with hunger.

Hastily lowering sail and making the *Zephyr* fast, we limped round a blank wall to the front entrance and saw ... the door off its hinges and the windows all blown in. The place was abandoned!

Neither of us spoke as we crawled through dank grass back to the *Zephyr*.

Getting out some damp biscuits and pouring out some cold water, we broke our fast, still in silence.

At length Brysdale remarked, as I had long suspected, that he wanted to go to church.

The remainder of that cruise is a happy souvenir of bright days, favouring breezes, and brilliant starlit nights, varied by a visit to Norwich Cathedral, a scramble round the massive ivy-clad walls of the old Roman camp at Burgh, and the tragedy of a young moorhen, which, seized before our eyes by a water-rat and dragged down a hole in the river bank, could be heard more and more faintly cheeping while on its dark and bitter journey from warmth and sunshine to the chill of eternal oblivion.

CHAPTER VII

Rats and Rabbits

It was a cheerless November evening and all the family was gathered round a blazing fire in the old rectory drawing-room.

'Please 'm, Mister Wicks wan t' see master Ollfer'.

I quickly joined old Trickler at the kitchen door, when, sinking his voice to a mysterious whisper, he tersely intimated: 'Jackson's er Pallin' temorrer mornin'. Eight er clock i' the dickey cart. Bring the dawg, tu polecats an' the jack', and then, apparently in a great hurry, he bustled out and closed the door, only, however, to instantly reopen it and say: 'Berrer bring a bite o' wittles an' a drop er suffen short, then I shornt het tu,' at the same time casually drawing the back of his hand across a toothless mouth.

Being extremely flattered by the importance of this unexpected invitation, I took the hint, and supplied Mr Wicks with a glass of beer, while promising that all should be in readiness at eight next morning.

Marky and I breakfasted by candlelight in the kitchen, and then taking two ferret bags of coarse sacking with a little straw at the bottom of each, I put the two small polecat-coloured rat ferrets into one and the big white rabbit jack-ferret into the other.

The contents of my game-bag were also overhauled: a ferret line with small leather collar for the jack, half a dozen purse-nets to put over rabbit holes, a pair of thick leather gloves for working amongst thorns, some bread and cheese and sandwiches, and two bottles of light draught ale, by way of something short.

It was not yet eight o'clock and very misty, when, with everything collected in readiness at the front gate, I made out Trickler, seated in his donkey cart, slowly approaching up the lane, with his little mongrel, Fanny, trotting in advance.

Without wasting time in vain salutations, I tossed my belongings into the cart, balanced myself beside Trickler on a board which served as seat, and we were away, heading for Palling at a good three miles an hour.

It gradually dawned on me that, with the exception of a narrow, long-handled rabbiting spade, none of Trickler's ordinary ferreting gear was in the cart, and on my hastily drawing his attention to the fact in belief that it had been forgotten, he bared two or three yellow stumps in a noiseless laugh before explaining in the light of a great joke that his ferrets being all laid up with scabbed feet, he thought I should like mine to have a chance, especially as, he added seriously, we should of course 'share and share alike' in all profits earned.

Needless to say I felt more honoured and more important than ever.

Arriving at Jackson's farm shortly after nine, Trickler drove into a ploughed field, unharnessed the donkey and turned him loose to forage round the hedges, and then shouldering ferrets, game-bag, and spade, we started up a loke in search of game, Marky and Fanny working both banks and sniffing at all rat-holes.

'Fanny seem ter saye there's suffen here,' said Trickler, tossing one of the small ferrets across the holl to a rat-hole behind a stub on the deek. 'Stan' yow right quite tegither', to me and the dogs.

One might have heard a pin drop for a good five minutes, when suddenly at the bottom of the holl there was a short, sharp squeak, and Marky was shaking the life out of a rat.

We had just returned to the strained silence of expectancy, when 'Lo-lo-lo, Lo-lo-lo, Lo-lo-lo', I yelled, giving chase to an enormous rat as he went hopping up the loke for all he was worth, but before the long-handled spade with which I was armed could be brought to bear, he had disappeared again into another hole.

Both dogs were, like myself, just too late, though each now stood motionless as a statue watching a hole, while old Trickler, having taken up the ferret from the first place, came briskly up on the opposite side and copt it over the hedge to me, when, the catch being successful, I turned it down where Mr Rat had just disappeared.

Half inside the hole, the ferret stood perfectly still for a few seconds, then slowly drew forward about three inches and stood still again, by which action I knew that the rat was quite close by; then in one flash it was gone, there was a rush, a snap, another short, sharp squeak, and all was over; this prize having fallen to Fanny.

After this, sport was dull for a time, but eventually the dogs came to a standstill over some flooring in a disused outhouse.

At first the ferret refused to go in, and when finally it did, there was immediately a most exciting rattling and thumping under the boards, and then it quickly reappeared 'currabout a rum 'un', in fact, it looked at first as though one eye were cut through.

Trickler pronounced it to be 'an old she-rat wi' a neast er young 'uns an' no ferret'll face 'em', and forthwith commenced to tear up the rotten boarding with his hands, when, on a plank being lifted, the rat sprang out, to be at once seized by both dogs and almost torn in two.

Having examined the victim, Trickler declared his diagnosis to be correct, and thrusting in an arm full length amongst cobwebs and loose earth, he presently drew out a rough, straw nest containing several hideous little rats not more than a day or two old.

We killed two more full grown 'uns in the same shed, and then availed ourselves of its shelter for lunch, which my host and partner pronounced to be 'fämeish', as he puffed great clouds from a tiny, jet-black clay, by way of an after-dinner smoke.

The fixed price for killing rabbits was ninepence a head, and for rats threepence, so that I calculated we had already earned fifteenpence, which meant sevenpence halfpenny each.

On making a re-start, we had to cross a stubble, when a rabbit jumped up at our very feet and was chased with piercing shrieks by Marky and Fanny, while Trickler and I followed as fast as possible with encouraging 'Lo-lo-lo, Lo-lo-los', till we got him aground in a big bank, thickly overgrown with furze and blackthorn, and having a deep water-ditch on one side.

It was a regular stronghold, honeycombed with old burrows, but as rabbits were then few and far between, we instituted elaborate siege operations in hopes of getting him out.

My six nets were pegged down over the most likely looking holes, while all others were carefully stopped.

The big jack having been got out of his bag, and the line fastened round his neck, he was turned down one of the holes, under a net.

At first he drew along very slowly with frequent stoppings, as we could tell by the line, and then suddenly shot forward, or 'stuck', while at the same moment I heard and caught sight of a rabbit struggling and jerking in a net on top of the bank.

Not being able to reach him because of the water-ditch, and fearing least he should escape, I aimed a terrific blow with the long-handled spade.

Trickler on the opposite side had also seen the netted rabbit, and not being hindered by the water-ditch, got his hand on to it just ahead of my spade.

I killed the rabbit stone dead, while Trickler set up an inarticulate howl: 'Ow-ow-ow, ow-ow-ow', followed by denunciations, interrupted luckily by need of instant action in rescuing from the dogs another rabbit which, fleeing before the jack, had also popped into a net.

Such good luck took all the venom out of Trickler's animosity, and beyond nursing his hand for a few minutes, uttering several growls to the effect that I might ha' done him a mischief, and strongly advising me to 'hev a keer', the storm passed; the more easily as tugs on the line revealed the pleasant fact that Master Jack was 'hard on' to yet another rabbit, which drew a delighted 'If that beant the masterpiece!' from my fellow hunter.

The 'masterpiece' took a lot of getting. If we killed the first two in three minutes, it took a good three hours to dig out the third.

By measuring the length of line still in hand, we could tell that the ferret was in about eight yards, while any doubt as to there being a rabbit was set at rest by putting one's head to the mouth of the hole and listening, when faint rumblings like the sound of distant thunder could be heard, and which could only be made by poor bunny struggling in the grip of the big white jack.

We dug holes into the bank at several places from six to eight yards ahead, but no trace of either ferret or line could be found, while those tell-tale rumblings had long since been silenced in the stillness of death. There was nothing for it but to follow the line.

My leather gloves now came in useful as I hacked and dug away amongst thorns and furze, scooping out spade-fuls of yellow earth which slid down over my boots into the water-ditch, till it was half filled up.

At the end of a couple of hours the place looked like a line of fresh earthworks, and I had eventually to knock off exhausted, clothes torn, face scratched, and wet through with perspiration, while apparently we were no nearer our quarry than at the very beginning.

Trickler again declared it to be a 'masterpiece', but this time with puzzled countenance.

Crawling into one of the openings till only his corduroys and hobnailed boots could be seen, he stayed there a long time listening, and, I believe, sniffing with his large fleshy nose.

Finally he drew back, all covered with yellow sand and clay, and, sitting on his heels, appeared to reflect deeply, while the little beadlike eyes ranged about, measuring distances.

After several minutes he got up, while I and the dogs watched in interested silence, crossed the ditch, stepped about two paces from the brow of the holl into the stubble, and planting his heel in the ground with great solemnity, said 'There'.

I couldn't believe it, for to get 'there' the rabbit-hole must lead from the bank deep down under the water-ditch and come up again in the field on the opposite side.

However, Trickler took the spade, made an opening, and after digging out about two feet of earth, went down on both knees, grubbed about with his hand, and suddenly produced before our astonished eyes a headless rabbit and the big white ferret, blinking and licking his chops.

His silent triumph was that of the *maestro*!

It was now late afternoon, so putting the jack back into his bag to dream of succulent rabbits' heads, we collected our gear and trailed back towards the farm-house, very pleased with the day's sport.

Hanging over the closed farmyard gate I suddenly noticed a thick-set, black-bearded, fierce-looking man, surmounted by a very large bowler hat and armed with a most formidable five-foot staff. This terrible-looking person was Farmer Jackson.

I felt myself change colour as the thought struck me that for some reason or other we were in for bad times, and was much relieved when he slowly pushed the gate open at our approach, while stating in the mildest of mild voices that he had just seen a rat on one of his wheat stacks.

Getting a long ladder and planting it where the rat had been seen, I was soon up with a small ferret, and popped it into a right fresh hole in the thatch, when instantly the rat made a bolt, and being armed with a long stick, I just swept him off the sloping thatch, to hear a thud twenty feet below as he struck the ground, where the waiting dogs instantly polished him off.

Farmer Jackson looked on in gloomy silence, though I suppose with satisfaction, for after taking possession of the three rabbits and counting the six rats, he handed Trickler three and ninepence without ado, and then strode slowly away.

The donkey was already waiting by the cart, as though tired of the ploughed field, so that in less than no time all was aboard and we were rattling homewards at full gallop.

'Short and sweet like a donkey's gallop' is an old saying both in Norfolk and Italy, and it was not long before we had to content ourselves with a trot, though altogether the journey home was much brisker than the journey out; after the manner of all donkeys.

My mind dwelt pleasantly on that three and ninepence, the half of which I felt would come in very handy, and could not refrain from telling Trickler so, but he must have been thinking of other things, for my remark passed unheeded, though he kept repeating to himself at intervals, 'We shornt git werry fat. We shornt git werry fat'; the purport of which I was at a loss to understand.

Having reached Hickling High Hill, a towering eminence of some three feet and without rival in that pancake-like country, Trickler heaved a heart-rending sigh (due, I thought, to agony from the injured hand), brought the donkey to a standstill in the middle of the road, and expressed his intention of 'squaring up, share and share alike'.

Spreading out the three and ninepence on his open left hand, he again remarked, 'We shornt git weery fat', and got to business.

'There's half a crown for my day's work', he said, picking up that sum with his right forefinger and thumb and returning it to his pocket, 'and a bob for the dickey and cart', similarly whisking off that amount, 'an' that leave trippence ter share an' share alike: tree ha'pence f'r yow an' tree ha'pence f'r me, just enow f'r half a nounce er baccy, an' we shornt git werry fat', ending up with a noiseless laugh and a confidential back-hand tap or two on my chest.

I took the lordly sum without enthusiasm, feeling that something was wrong, though at the same time knew such thoughts were quite unworthy of me as traitorous to the exalted position I held in the confidence of Mr Wicks.

The greatest thing I ever knew in the rat line was the killing one morning of a hundred and ninety in Jarrot's barn.

It happened in this wise.

Mr Jarrott was the parish miller, owning an eight-storied, flour-grinding windmill, besides farming about forty acres in his own right.

He was a short, thick-set, long-bearded man of great physical strength, an expert gardener and fruit grower, renowned locally for his 'larnin' ', of stubborn, unyielding disposition, and the father of four handsome daughters and a son of my own age, named Nester.

Nester and I were great friends, so that in his company I had the run of the mill, the fruit gardens, the farm, and the *rats*.

It was the best farmyard for sport that ever was, so that with Marky and my ferrets, Nester and I never failed to make a good bag.

A row of pig-sties was the hottest corner, when putting

the ferrets in at one end, the rats would move off before them like a shoal of roach playing on the surface of the Broad, weaving themselves out of one hole and in at another – for the old wooden flooring was perforated like a colander – till having reached the last stye, there would be a wild helter-skelter before the approaching ferrets; and it was then that we got in our fine work with tough blackthorn sticks ere the rats could reach the barn, for which they always seemed to make.

One day we would kill five or six out of these sties, and yet on the next day there always seemed to be just as many more. It was really very much like the widow's cruse!

Owing to the criminal rascality of whichever political party was then in power (according to Mr Jarrott), the price of barley had fallen considerably below what it should have been, so that being a man of 'stubborn, unyielding disposition', he had stacked one season's barley crop in his barn, with the sworn intention of keeping it there till prices had fully recovered.

After three years the desired figures were quoted, and orders were issued to turn the barley over preparatory to threshing it with flails.

Drawn by instinct and local knowledge, Marky and I joined Nester at the turning.

Rats! Rats! Rats! How they flew in all directions! Marky fought and slew, sticks slashed, forks jabbed!

The battle over, our victims filled two bushel skeps with their mangled corpses; while the barley . . . yes, the barley? . . . well, what there was left of it, even the pigs wouldn't touch.

One of my numerous harbours of refuge was a pleasant

farm about two miles to the eastward, at the end of a long and lonely lane.

The farmer and his wife had both turned seventy and were of the old school, hard work about the land and in the stockyards being the master's sole thought, while his good lady took delight in keeping the house a picture of cleanliness and comfort, in paying careful attention to poultry, and in making the best butter for miles round.

A son and a daughter, no longer in their teens, made the family complete.

When the burden of lessons or other afflictions proved intolerable, to Farmer Lubin's I would fly, always sure of a kindly welcome, especially from the old lady; while riding the big farm horses, chasing pigs, hunting for nests of stray hens, and turning the churn on butter-making days, afforded most excellent diversion.

Speaking of pigs, the remembrance of my first utter discomfiture in life comes painfully back.

In Mr Lubin's orchard was a large tree of small but delicious chiselly pears, of which I was free to eat all wind-falls.

When pears were in, a visit to the orchard was one of my first duties on arriving at the farm.

One day, however, I was forestalled, finding an enormous sow, which had got in through a gap in the hedge, just munching the last of what I naturally considered my property.

Bent on vengeance, the willing assistance of a small boy who chopped turnips for the bullocks was enlisted.

While with heavy bludgeon upraised all ready to strike, I waited beyond the hedge directly in front of the gap, he was to chase Madame Sow out of the orchard.

After about two minutes of suspense there was a scuffle, a resounding whack, a squeal, three or four quick, sharp grunts, and the sow, apparently not weighing less than fifty tons, shot through the gap like a torpedo, taking me amidships with her pointed, cast-iron snout, and hurling my limp, winded, and speechless form a good three yards to the rear, without ever having had a chance to get in a single blow.

Moral: 'Never despise an enemy, be it only a tame sow'.

To repeat: Mrs Lubin ever gave me a most kindly welcome, in fact, I think I must have held a warm corner in the old lady's heart, for she always invited me to join in their evening meal, and the remembrance of those pleasant family gatherings, the snow-white cloth, the hot, strong tea, the lovely cream, the fresh eggs, and that delicious buttered toast, has followed me to the ends of the earth.

One evening at table Mr George Lubin said he wished to consult me on important business, my age at that time being about six.

He said the number of rabbits on the farm was increasing so rapidly that his father would really be very much obliged to me if I could bring ferrets and dog, and perhaps my brothers with their guns, and kill them off.

Now here was something like an invitation! *My* invitation.

What a cleaning of guns and starving of ferrets there was for a couple of days, and then we moved off in a solid body.

There was no hanky-panky about it: *I* was in command. *I* showed them where to go, *I* told them what to do, and by noon we had killed six beauties; and were just thinking of our bread and cheese, when Mr George arrived to say that dinner was ready.

This was overwhelming, but then I didn't entertain my four hungry brothers every day in the week, so headed the procession towards the house.

What a spread there was, and everything first class! I can't remember all the things, but I can still see Miss Lubin bringing in a splendid plum-pudding all steaming hot.

In the afternoon we killed eight more, making a total of fourteen, and having taken them to the house and thanked our kind entertainers, prepared to trudge home, when Mr George said he happened to be going our way with his square cart and could give us a lift.

We all packed in, and I drove while the lane was straight, Mr George only taking command at corners; and when we got down at the rectory, three brace of rabbits were unexpectedly handed to us out of the cart by way of a present.

I felt that things had been done on a grand scale.

There has long been a handsome Mrs George Lubin, and a grandson named after the little boy who used to chase pigs forty years ago, while the old lady only passed away on the 26th April, 1909, at the somewhat advanced age of one hundred and eight.

The wheels of Geoffrey's square cart crunch-crunch-crunched through ice-covered puddles, as with guns and plenty of cartridges, we bowled along the Cancer *en route* for Waxham Hall.

'Splendid mornin'.'

'Splendid. Just right.'

The rime began to lift towards nine o'clock, showing

lofty sand dunes, beyond which murmured occasionally the sea, as though waking from its sleep.

Keen, bracing air, sunshine breaking through, and anticipation of a good day's rabbiting, drew from Geoffrey a few bars in deepish bass of 'I stood on the bridge at midnight.'

Past the Lownd Farm, through Palling Street, and then on to the Hall, where Crow the keeper was waiting with several bags of ferrets, his dog Gip and two or three farm hands.

Looking something like Pickwick's fat, sleepy boy, Crow removed a short, black clay about half an inch from his thick lips and remarked by way of salutation: 'There's a bowtiful mornin',' to which we readily assented.

The young squire lured us to his den for refreshment after our early drive, and then everything being ready, a start was made for the marram-covered sand-hills, the landward side of which was alive with rabbits.

First, we all spread out and walked line abreast to the end of our ground in search of any rabbits that might be playing about, the squire at the foot of the dunes, Geoffrey half-way up, and myself on top, from where I had on the one side a lovely panorama of glittering, ship-covered waves, and on the other a perfectly flat country reaching away to the horizon without eminence of any kind. Averaging perhaps fifty feet in height, by one hundred and twenty wide at the base, that insignificant thread of semi-artificial sand-dunes yet stood as frontier between the mighty realms of land and sea.

Half a dozen bunnies were quickly bowled over, though one which I had apparently killed stone dead revived in most miraculous manner just as Crow was about to pick it up, and disappeared like a flash down a near-by hole. Then retracing our steps to some large burrows, the real business began.

Purse-nets were placed over all start-holes that could be seen although we knew there were plenty more hidden by the thick two-foot high marram; the guns took up positions facing outwards different ways, so as not to interfere with each other's shooting; while Crow untied two of the bags and loosed six coped ferrets down the main burrow.

Formerly ferrets were coped by the cruel, if simple, method of sewing their mouths up, that is, stitching the lips together, so that when released without line down large burrows, they could only attack with claws and scare out the rabbits, without being able to kill and then 'lay up' after a good meal.

Crow's ferrets were all coped with miniature muzzles of stout twine, but tied on so tight that anything else would certainly have died, whereas those bloodthirsty little animals seemed quite oblivious to what must have been excruciating agony, and scuttled gaily after the rabbits in vain hopes of making a kill.

For the first few minutes there was dead silence, then suddenly a perfect hurricane of rabbits seemed to leap forth: nets jerked about with the vain struggles of enmeshed victims, we gunners blazed away till our barrels got almost too hot to hold, and even Gip caught one or two.

Rabbits can go as quick as hares for about two hundred yards, and when they have been well scratched by the sharp claws of coped ferrets, as well as terrified by close proximity to such dreaded foes, they quit their invaded burrows at almost incredible speed, and seeing that generally they follow well beaten runs through the long marram, when only flash-like glimpses of them can be caught, it requires a good snapshot to kill anything at all.

By noon we had shot six or seven each, and missed probably twice as many more, while the bag from all sources numbered thirty-five.

Seated on the sunny side of a bank, we were just finishing an excellent lunch, when the sleepy Crow suddenly sprang to his feet, gibbering unintelligibly and executing a sort of cake-walk before our astonished eyes, while throwing off coat, waistcoat, and other garments in rapid succession.

Inspection showed that he had been sitting on a pishameres' nest, and the little ants, doubtless warmed by generous heat from that massive bulk, had passed by hundreds to the person of their unconscious oppressor.

In the afternoon we followed similar tactics, the sport, if anything, being even better, though towards evening Gip disappeared, and not for some time did we discover that the poor dog was buried alive, as having crept far down a large burrow in pursuit of a wounded rabbit, the sand had suddenly caved in.

We dug frantically in turns for a good hour, hopes of finding the dog alive falling lower and lower, and when finally we did reach the buried treasure, it merely shook the sand out of its coat and went on hunting just as though nothing had happened; a case of sheer ingratitude, and we all felt it as such.

We knocked off with forty to our credit since lunch, making a total bag of seventy-five: a good day's sport for anyone.

CHAPTER VIII

Winter Sports

THE sun set in a frosty glow, while tiny spikes of ice shooting across a handcupful of water placed in an exposed position by the pump, made us rub our hands with glee, for at length the time of skates and pussy was at hand.

After dark, we would pop out o' doors a score of times to strike matches in the keen, still air, and by their light inspect an ancient thermometer, our hopes rising or falling inversely with the readings of that scientific instrument, supplementing such observations by tappings on the now thin layer of ice in the handcup, as well as by the rattle of cart-wheels in the lane and their tell-tale crish-crunshings through frozen puddles.

On awaking next morning and peeping above the coverlets of our warm beds, we would gaze with delight at the lovely flowers, graceful ferns and glistening patterns with which Jack Frost had adorned our windows during the night, and then having dressed in frantic haste while puffing out great clouds of white steam, there would be a wild helter-skelter up the lane to a farmyard pond, to inspect both quality and thickness of the ice.

During the day skates would be got out, rubbed up, oiled and taken to the blacksmith's grindstone to be sharpened, while the house was thoroughly searched for straps of any kind.

Excitement rose higher and higher with each hour of

frosty weather, the tension becoming wellnigh intolerable, till on the third evening we felt so certain of skating next day that we could scarcely go to bed; and when we awoke to find a damp drizzle apparently set in for good, the reaction was overpowering; in our sleep we had been treacherously betrayed, and the disaster was of colossal magnitude.

Before noon, however, the drizzle turned to sleet, and then from sleet to snow, which silently fell and fell in downy flakes and in ever increasing quantities, till ground, roofs, hedges, trees, all lay still beneath a cloak of dazzling whiteness, some six inches thick.

Snow-balling took the place of the game of elephants, with this difference, that instead of carrying on operations only amongst ourselves, we would combine, waylay and mercilessly pelt any luckless mortal who approached the house or passed along the lane.

A fat butcher had long been the favourite butt of my brothers.

Arriving at a rattling trot, this worthy would pull up with a jerk, descend as briskly as possible from the cart, tie up his pony to the railings and waddle round a corner of the house to the kitchen door in search of orders or to deliver meat.

Now was the time. In a second that luckless pony was in the hands of lurking Redskins, who, their fell purpose wrought, would vanish into ambush again as quickly and silently as they had come.

On returning to his cart, the butcher on one occasion found the pony had been taken out, the shafts passed through a gate, and the animal then put to again, so that the cart was on one side of the gate and the pony on the other. Neither the butcher's remarks while putting matters straight, nor the expression of his countenance, escaped notice.

On another occasion the pony was found put to wrong way about, with head towards the cart and reins fastened to his tail.

On yet another occasion, finding all well, the butcher briskly mounted to his seat, snatched up whip and reins, gave the pony a cut, and had the pleasure of seeing him jump clean out of the shafts, both traces having somehow become mysteriously unhooked.

In this wise the butcher had become an inveterate enemy, wherefore, snow being plentiful, it behoved me to show what I could do, and strike a blow in the common weal.

Waiting round the corner of the house with a snowball as large and as hard as a Dutch cheese, I discharged it point blank into the enemy's full-blown face, and turned to flee. Unfortunately, my foot slipped on the frozen snow, and before I could gather myself together again, the butcher's eighteen-stone bulk had fallen upon me, while his hands, possessing the solidity and weight of hams, smacked my head till it buzzed and hummed, rubbed my face in the snow till I gasped for breath, and finally picked me up and hurled me head over heels into a snow-drift.

The jeers of my brothers mingling with the execrations of the butcher, hastened my decision to thenceforth rigidly abstain from all interference in the quarrels of others.

What games we had in the newly fallen snow! Hare and hounds was a strong favourite. One of the elder boys would be given ten minutes' start, and then the others, accompanied by various village friends, would follow on his tracks: across fields, over banks and water-ditches, through hedges, along lokes and through gardens. It was immaterial to us where the tracks led as we followed in a straggling pack floundering waist deep through snow-drifts or crashing through thin and rotten ice on slads and marshes, till after a four or five mile run, we would all reach home in an exhausted and sodden state.

Once we made a snow-house with walls some seven feet high by two feet thick, all built of enormous snowballs.

Taking an ordinary snowball, we would roll it round and round on the grass till it had grown to the size of a bushel, when it was placed in position, and in this manner, row upon row, the walls were raised, pierced by only one small aperture, flush with the ground, which served as window and door combined.

For the roof, we laid rough poles across the tops of the walls, then brushwood and straw on the poles, surmounting all with a thick layer of snow piled up to a sharp point; and the structure was complete.

It was a noble edifice, though somewhat dark, damp and cold inside, for which reason we lighted on the floor a big fire of dry sticks to make things more comfortable.

Having forgotten to make a chimney, we were all but blinded and suffocated by the smoke, which seemed to be of a peculiarly pungent nature, and no sooner were the dry sticks well alight, than flames shot up to the roof, ignited the straw, the brushwood and the rough poles, which in turn melted the snow piled up above, bringing down cascades of water and volumes of steam, till we were constrained to beat an ignominious retreat from that blazing smoking, raining, steaming, hissing cauldron, and to gaze mournfully from the outside on its reeking, melting destruction – as did Napoleon on Moscow.

During cold winters, when snow covered the ground, wild birds of all kinds became wonderfully tame, oftentimes collecting in large numbers close round the house in search of shelter and food.

Blackbirds, thrushes, robins and other domestic songbirds were free from molestation, such being father's wish, but sparrows, larks, wood-pigeons and fieldfare were considered fair game, and of these good bags were made both with trap and gun.

Large flocks of larks and fieldfare would often alight in snow-covered turnips fields, when following along the ridges, and passing by sound turnips, they would work down through the snow to any soft or decaying roots, and satisfy their hunger by pecking out the pulpy interiors, until only the tough rinds were left.

Firing along a ridge into the brown, a dozen or more could often be killed at one shot.

For sparrows, we would set traps made of four bricks, three for the sides and front, and one for the lid, which last, propped up on end by two pieces of thin stick set with all the delicacy of a hair trigger, would fall the instant a sparrow touched them on seeking to devour inviting breadcrumbs with which the trap had been baited.

Another and more effective plan was to sweep a small place clear of snow, get a four-foot sieve from the stables, and turning it upside down, set one edge up with a foot-long stick, to which was attached one end of a very long string. The other end of this string would be led through a small hole or crack into an outhouse, and there we would wait and watch until one, two, or perhaps three sparrows had hopped under the raised sieve for the crumbs or grain temptingly displayed there, when, smartly pulling the string and so jerking away the stick, the sieve would fall, and we would rush out to secure our entrapped victims.

On a good day, we would get as many as thirty or forty small birds, all told; and then what a plucking and cleaning there would be in the gun-room, until the thirty or forty poor little carcasses were all neatly arranged in one large pan, so to be roasted for a hunters' feast.

Speaking from experience, sparrow-pie is a delicacy by no means to be despised.

Presently frost would set in again, and the water being already perished, in three or four days the Broad would be 'laid', that is, all frozen over.

Each armed with a pair of old-fashioned wooden skates, and my elder brothers wearing knee-boots of stout leather, we would set out for the Broad immediately after breakfast and try the ice in shallow places round its edges.

The heavy wearers of knee-boots would go first, for even if they broke through, it did not matter, while if the ice would only just bear them, then, relying on the old verdict,

> *Bend she break*
> *Crack she hold,*

I could fearlessly launch my featherweight almost everywhere upon the quaking surface.

Skirting the shore, we would follow each other in an extended line, and while from the rear I could watch the black, frozen surface bend and roll beneath each of those in front, whose skates would oftentimes cut quite through,

I myself had the sensation of always skating uphill, owing to the thin, sheer ice settling down an inch or two beneath my weight, putting me, as it were, at the bottom of a tiny moving valley, the side of which I was ever trying to ascend, to an accompaniment of rending cracks, merry as the sound of jingling sleigh-bells and driver's ringing whip.

Probably a few fishermen would join us on these pioneer trips, but not till the morrow, or the day after, would skating become general, when hundreds of all classes flocked down from the whole countryside.

There were no acmes or spring skates in those days, every one wearing the old-fashioned wooden ones, while many boys and fishermen had not even straps, their skates being lashed on with yards and yards of string, which, on becoming stretched and loose, was tightened up by driving in wooden pegs or wedges between it and the boot, till finally each of the skater's feet resembled a miniature faggot.

What a long, cold job it was putting on skates! Seated on the ice or frozen bank, boring deep holes into hard heels with a small gimlet and numb fingers, screwing the skates round and round, and then securing them either with straps or with string and wedges, of which last whole pocketfuls would be carried by way of reserve.

Thirty years ago very few ladies skated, it not being considered quite the thing, so that the performers consisted almost wholly of men and boys, each armed with a thick stick, and who, when not tearing along, heads well down and arms widely swinging, in a long string one behind the other, looking much like an enormous centipede, would play a kind of ice hockey, known locally as 'pussy'.

No sides were chosen for this game, and there were no goals and no rules, the sole aim and object of half a hundred players being to smite the pussy, a knob of wood about as large as a potato, as hard and as often as possible, so that it skimmed madly to and fro over the ice from one direction to another, every one racing after it with loud cries of 'Our wipe! our wipe!'

Some of the fishermen's pussy sticks were like young trees, so that it was well not to get a 'wipe' either from them or from the pussy after it had been struck, as it went whistling for a quarter of a mile across the ice.

Every one kept on the move, following up the pussy like a pack of hounds, and starting after it at full speed as soon as it came in their direction, yelling 'Our wipe! our wipe!' so that continually there were neck and neck races, with a clashing of sticks, showers of white ice dug up by sharp skate-heels driven deep in to steady the strikers, encouraging shouts of 'Go een! *go-o* een! *go-o-o* een!' and oftentimes some thumping falls; all followed with the keenest interest and excitement, till a moment later the pussy, whizzing back through the players, would send every one off again in a new direction, to the invariable music of 'Our wipe! our wipe!'

In long, severe winters, ice on the Broad would sometimes be almost a foot thick, when I have seen upon it such things as pony-sledges, tents and fires; and at such times Old Tom would break open large places, called wakes, for the swans, which would otherwise sit, waddle and slide about on the slippery surface in most helpless fashion; and as one night's sharp frost would freeze these wakes up again, the ice had to be broken daily in order to keep open water.

Frozen out elsewhere, coots and wildfowl would by night join the swans in these wakes, and from one cause or another, in the morning a good number of them would at times be found frozen fast into the newly-formed ice, from which, however, the swans were strong enough to extricate themselves, and on one occasion I saw a young farmer secure nearly a score of mallard, poachard and coots by means of his dog, which, creeping gingerly over the quaking layer of new ice, forcibly dragged the stark, ill-fated birds one by one from their frozen beds, and retrieved them into the hands of his waiting master.

When the ice was very pure and transparent, we would skate quietly over the shallows, until, maybe, we saw a large pike in difficulties, being almost nipped between the upper and nether millstones of ice and weedy bottom. Closely following his floundering efforts to escape, we would rain terrific blows on the ice just over his head, until stunned by the concussion, he gave up the struggle, and was quickly secured through a hole broken in the ice above him.

Oftentimes a heavy fall of snow would cover the ice to a depth of several inches, which, while putting a stop to general skating, was yet a godsend to large numbers of men and boys thrown out of work by the severe weather, for they would assemble on the Broad in strength with shovels and brooms and clear fine roadways in all directions, along which merry, chattering skaters would glide, and only too pleased to 'remember the sweepers'.

The Rarverand was also squire of the parish, and coursing being one of his favourite forms of sports, from about the middle of December till well on into February, he would hold a coursing meet once a fortnight, that is,

provided the weather remained open, for in case of hard
frost no coursing was possible, as the iron ground would
have cut and ruined the dogs' feet, to say nothing of
possible broken legs.

Activity would arrive with: 'Master's compliments,
and would the young gentlemen drive the covers on
Wednesday morning at eleven o'clock?'

The young gentlemen would, and Activity having
refreshed, carried back word to that effect.

Guns were cleaned, supplies of powder, shot, wads and
patches procured, and on Wednesday morning we
marched up to the Vicarage in a body, finding there one
or two other guns, and being welcomed by Gamekeeper
Water Will, with Game-pie and a few lads as beaters.

The Rarverand usually did not appear, and so without
more ado, we would start for the coverts.

Taking the long Town Wood as an example, the guns
quietly lined up across it about a third of the way down,
while the beaters, entering at the top-end, by loud shouting and a great tapping of sticks, drove all before them
towards the guns.

Waiting breathlessly at our stations, we would presently become aware of hares and rabbits hopping nerv-
ously towards us, stopping every few yards to sit up and
listen with their long, sensitive ears, and then hopping
stealthily towards us again, while wood-pigeons and an
occasional pheasant whizzed overhead through the trees.

Our business was to shoot only the rabbits and so
frighten the hares out of the wood, when, taking to the
fields and marshes, they would make forms and lay out for
several days before venturing back to their disturbed
coverts.

It was very like a small coot shooting. 'Bang bang, bang', rang out half a dozen shots almost simultaneously, when pandemonium immediately reigned amongst the woodland folk, unmolested hares darting like arrows towards the open country, rabbits scurrying to and fro in vain attempts to conceal themselves in undergrowth and bracken but only to roll over and over beneath storms of leaden hail, while numbers of terrified blackbirds and thrushes, uttering shrill notes of alarm, fled in all directions.

My station proved a very good one, and I had already accounted for half a dozen rabbits, when either a rabbit or a hare moved stealthily into some bracken.

To shoot a hare was, I knew, a crime of the blackest; but on the other hand, to allow a rabbit to slip through my fingers and fall to another's gun, was a disaster, and so, as I had to decide at once, I elected to take my chance, and fired: whereupon, to my horror, a fine hare leaped six feet into the air and fell back stone dead.

A vision of the Rarverand's dire wrath caused me to turn first hot and then cold, so that when the beaters came up and Water Will and Gamepie began picking up the dead rabbits which were lying about in all directions, I hesitated to make a clean breast of my sin till too late.

Water Will and Game-pie simultaneously came upon the dead hare, and I awaited the end of all things. To my astonishment, however, they merely looked at each other, looked at me, carelessly trod some bracken over their find as if to conceal it, and passed on to other things; though presently getting me alone, they assured me that 'If the Rarverand only knew, it 'ud be a bad day for all on us', and that if I wished to be saved, the only thing to do was to keep strict silence about the dreadful deed: to which, of course, I very readily assented, while earnestly thanking them for such thoughtful kindness.

The first drive resulted in twenty-five rabbits, and then the guns moved on to fresh positions, till all the wood was thoroughly scoured, and not a hare, I believe, remained in it.

At the beginning of the season only one covert was driven for a coursing meet, as it yielded hares enough, so that our sport was all over in about two hours, when we returned to the Vicarage with from fifty to sixty rabbits.

The Rarverand came out to see the bag, delighting us with full approval, while 'Bravo, little 'un!' followed on Water Will's unsolicited declaration that I personally had accounted for eleven head, and then my blood ran cold when the Rarverand asked me point-blank whether I had not managed to shoot a hare in mistake for a rabbit.

Utterly dumbfounded, I was unable to cudgel up any reply before Water Will interposed with a joking 'Th 'ole hares knew tu much ter give our young master the chance, du more'n likerly he'd a kilt half a dozen', which drew a roar of laughter from the Rarverand, dutifully echoed by all present, and the situation was saved.

I never heard of that hare again, but have often wondered what Water Will and Game-pie did with it!

By ten o'clock on Friday morning, that is, two days later, the Vicarage was besieged by all sorts and conditions of men, boys, horses and vehicles, while dozens of greyhounds, led about singly or in couples, at frequent intervals set up sharp yelpings of impatience and excitement.

Old Farmer Heeley, who, from the back of a sedate and

reliable nag, always officiated as judge, and who, with his portly person, full voice, red face and enormous purple nose, was of the type so faithfully portrayed by Caldecott, solemnly ambled and cantered about with an air of absolute invincibility.

The slipper, a lithe, active man arrayed in pink, bustled to and fro, followed by the admiring gaze of all; though by far the most important personage present was Activity, who, while his master held open house within, slowly passed from group to group in the stone-paved yard, with a 'Confound the dogs!' here, and a 'Dimme!' there, as though to the manner born.

Many of my village friends earned as much as sixpence or a shilling a day by leading either one or a couple of greyhounds, until wanted for the slips.

These greyhounds were held in leashes, the long, leather leads of which had running nooses at the end, to be slipped over the forearm, so that there should be no chance of the dogs breaking away when coursed hares passed close by, though I have often seen boys and even men jerked off their feet and dragged some considerable distance; in fact, I have been dragged a hundred yards or so myself, more than once, for naturally it was my one idea to lead a greyhound or even two, whenever I could get Activity to allow it, and not for the high wages paid, but purely for the honour and glory.

Excitement grew and grew till suddenly at about half past ten there would be a stampede out of the Vicarage gate and up Dairy-house Lane, with greyhounds straining at the leash, and the Rarverand, Farmer Heeley on horseback, the red-coated slipper with a couple of dogs already in the slips, and an *omnium gatherum* of those constituting themselves the 'knobs' of the neighbourhood, marching in front.

Presently the merry throng passed out of the lane through a gate held open by Water Will into the fourteen acres, when the *élite* took up favourable positions to view the sport, while the rest of us marched in line-abreast up the field, the slipper slightly in advance, and a bright sun rolling away the last of the morning mist.

Almost immediately 'Ser-hoe', came from Old Trimmer, and the whole line halted, until the slipper having led his dogs into a favourable position, said, 'Put her up', whereupon Old Trimmer made a rapid advance, apparently at nothing, till up sprang a splendid hare from under his very feet.

The eager greyhounds, a black and a big brindle, strained frantically at the slips, while the slipper eased them as much as possible by running till he judged 'Sally' had been allowed law enough, about eighty yards, and then slipped.

It was a large barley stubble or new-lay, and as smooth as a cricket field, so there was nothing to hinder the view.

Straight down the field the fleet-footed trio fled till within twenty yards of the hedge, when poor puss was overtaken, and, to avoid those gleaming fangs, which, as though steered by twirling, whip-like tails, followed with unerring aim, had to double this way and twist that, each time momentarily gaining a little ground, for being much lighter and shorter of body than her pursuers, she could turn rather more quickly.

It was a splendid course, the hare gradually working her way back the whole length of the field, with the greyhounds stretching out till their briskets almost swept the ground, and their lightning footsteps smiting the damp soil with hollow slap, the black and the brindle alternately showing in front.

With eyes and ears all alert to catch every movement of her pursuers, as well as to descry any avenue of escape, the hare made frantic efforts to reach a gateway which led to the Town Wood and safety. Straight through the spectators, who, with cries of 'Clear the gate, tegither!' and 'Go it, old gal!' fell back so as to give the hard-pressed hare every chance, it looked at one time as though she would succeed, when a false twist threw her, with a heart-rending, despairing cry, almost like that of a human soul in agony, right into the jaws of the big brindle, and her final course was run; whereon Farmer Heeley declared the black to be winner on points, Game-pie bustled up to stretch the victim's neck, huddle it by piercing a hole in one hind leg and drawing the other through it, and then triumphantly sling it on a thick stick over his shoulder, while the greyhounds were again coupled in the leash and led off to await their turn for another course.

As often as not, however, the hare would escape, for if she could find a hard, level path, slightly uphill, the dogs would quickly be left behind; or if any kind of cover, such as a copse, clumps of furze, rushes or osier beds could be reached, she was safe, for greyhounds always chase by sight and never by scent; while sometimes the dogs themselves came to grief.

I once saw a hard-pressed hare clear a good-sized marsh drain, which both her pursuers also simultaneously leaped, though one greyhound, having taken off too soon, struck his head against the far bank and rolled over stone dead with a broken neck, while the other suddenly lost all pace, and presently returned limping on three legs, when inspection showed that at that fatal jump he had drawn a toenail, and, I believe, had eventually to be destroyed.

At one o'clock a pony-cart would arrive with lunch, when new penny-rolls with large pieces of good, strong cheese were handed out to one and all by Activity, who also poured forth welcome ale from big stone bottles, and finally, exercising the discretion of a Chief Justice, would single out a few favoured ones for delicious sausage rolls: and I was seldom overlooked.

During the afternoon sport was continued, marshes, ploughs and stubbles all holding plenty of hares, so that the total number killed was generally between twenty and thirty.

There was no betting at these private meets, nor were any prizes offered: it was sport pure and simple, and better coursing I have never seen.

Village choirs are not what they were thirty years ago.

I remember one which sang to the strains of a barrel-organ, cranked by a stone-deaf sexton.

This barrel-organ was so old and worn that not infrequently when in the middle of a hymn it would stop playing, though the organist being 'hard er hearin' ' would fail to notice the omission and crank steadily on, and then suddenly, when the choir had sung on perhaps half a line, it would recommence playing where it had left off, creating confusion worse confounded.

I once heard a jovial Jack Tar deliberately sing one line behind our choir all the way through a hymn: but whether for mischief's sake, or merely from excess of 'spirits', I never knew.

In the choir of Waxham cum Palling were strapping

coastguardsmen, life-boatmen, fishermen and various old sea-dogs, together with their wives and children, to say nothing of a fair sprinkling of landsmen, the total number rising and falling with the time of year, and who, to the accompaniment of a little old harmonium played by my sister, could fairly make the welkin ring.

Once started on a favourite tune, the vibrant notes of wooden-leg Podler, the sweet contralto of the village belle, the fluty tenor of that jovial coastguard, and the growling bass of a six-foot teamster, wove themselves in and out of, led firmly on, and yet bound together a full-throated, almost rollicking stream of praise, not only from the choir, but also from the whole seafaring congregation, the like of which, in these days of surpliced youth, is but seldom heard.

In winter-time, when snow was on the ground, fierce gales blew and fishermen had all made up, the choir was at its best, in fettle as well as in numbers; for did not the great social event of the whole year, the 'Singers' Feast', take place a short time after Christmas!

On Christmas Eve the 'singers', as the choir was always called, went round to all the principal houses to sing carols, when, besides being overwhelmed with hospitality, they would collect subscriptions towards the Singers' Feast.

The feast was held in the old schoolroom, a long, low, narrow building with brick floor, few windows, and only one small ventilation hole through the thatched roof.

As each singer was allowed to bring one or two guests, the choir at Christmas-time swelled to huge proportions, so that finally almost the whole village would either be at the feast itself, or at least turn up in Sunday best immediately after dinner to join in the games, songs, dancing and general merrymaking.

Old 'Long Tom' Brown, a cavernous giant of some six feet six, had nothing whatever to do with singing, either in church or out, but as he could *eat his length in sausages* any day, his presence at the feast went without saying, and we boys would struggle for near-by seats in order to get a good view of the prowess of such a redoubtable champion.

The *menu* was of simple grandeur: first, delicious Norfolk dumplings and beef gravy; then mountains of prime roast beef and boiled mutton, backed up by potatoes, turnips, carrots, and horse-radish and washed down with good six-ale; while the 'sweets' course was represented solely by plum-puddings – lashins of 'em – and brandy sauce; to all of which cheese, celery and good old pickled onions put a fitting coping-stone.

What a row of healthy, happy faces beamed on either side of that long, narrow table; never again, alas, shall I see the like. Old folks, middle-aged couples, blue guern-seyed young fishermen with their pretty sweethearts, giggling girls and boys.

Father having taken position at one end of the festive board, and the officer of coastguards, a Crimean veteran than whom a better man never lived, at the other, grace was sung by all standing; after which but little was heard for the next half hour beyond a cheerful clatter of knives and forks.

Long Tom in private life passed as a silent man, though on Singers' Feast nights his eyes gleamed at the steaming joints with a fierceness which fully took the place of speech, and told of long fasting by way of preparation for the great event.

After wasting fully half a minute with a fork and blunt table-knife as an offering to polite manners, he suddenly drew a shut-knife from his trousers' pocket, opened its razor-like blade, and with its sharp point pitched plateful after plateful of roast beef into his trap-like mouth with the regularity of a steam dredger.

After a while, the good cheer told and tongues were unloosened. What a jolly, shouting, laughing, joking gathering it was! What a satire on dyspeptic millionaires!

Long Tom worked silently, unceasingly, and with great rapidity from the very start till everyone else had quite finished, and then spearing and whisking between his teeth one last pickled onion, with a heavy sigh regretfully closed his knife and returned it to his pocket, drew the back of a huge hand slowly across his mouth, and, amidst a general chorus of 'Long Tom's done', dinner was over.

Willing hands soon cleared away not only plates and dishes, but also the table itself, leaving the whole room free for dancing, while forms and chairs were ranged all round the walls.

Snow-white clay pipes, called 'church-wardens', having stems three feet long and each tipped with red sealing-wax by way of mouth-piece, were handed round to all smokers, together with half-ounce packets of black shag.

The little old harmonium was wheeled into position, lads and lassies exchanged meaning glances, the school-mistress seated herself at the instrument, and in a trice we were footing it to the wailing, wind-blown strains of a polka.

As already stated, the floor was of brick, much worn in places and not exactly springy, though that was to be

expected and of no particular consequence. Right across
the middle, however, there was a sandy space four or five
feet wide, devoid of bricks altogether, such doubtless
having been kicked up and broken by the daily tread of
countless little hobnailed boots.

Over brick floor, down a couple of inches into the sandy
valley, and then up again on to brick floor, marked each
journey from one end of the room to the other; but what
of that, it only added to the fun, and, I must add, the dust,
for presently the whole room was a blur of sandstorm and
tobacco smoke, through which the harmonium still
squeaked blindly on, candles stared red and dim, and
phantom couples waxed and waned.

The polka over, Podler luxuriously stretched out his
wooden leg towards the fire and rendered, 'The Wonderful Crocodile', which reptile, besides being a matter of
some three hundred miles in length, was also the possessor
of a befitting shell, all of which the singer knew through
personal, Jonah-like explorations; and then being encored,
he favoured us with:

> The Cast-iron man
> Who bought a steam gun,
> An' went a shootin'
> Alonger his son, etc., etc.

detailing at great length the most unique and thrilling
adventures imaginable.

Then followed a schottische, to the merry strains of a
concertina exceedingly well played; then a song from 'the
prettiest girl in the room', who saddened us with that fine
old ballad, 'The Mistletoe Bough'; then the old-fashioned
cushion dance, with its attendant forfeits; a nigger song,

'So early in the mornin' '; and so on, dance uninter-
ruptedly following song, with frequent handings round of
oranges, slices of delicious cold plum-pudding, nuts, cake,
tea, coffee, etc., till well after midnight, when 'Sir Roger
de Coverley' brought a strenuous and thoroughly enjoyable evening to a befitting close: an evening when all the
parish, parson and clerk, master and man, girls and boys,
met in kindliest and most innocent enjoyment, and when
the old message of 'Peace on Earth, Goodwill towards
Man' seemed almost a reality, and came much nearer
home to me than it ever has done in after years.

Present times may be more prosperous, new manners
may be more fine, while 'larnin' ', we know, is nowadays
required of all — still, give *me* the Old; for through long
years of lonely exile, memories of old times, old ways, old
friends ever bore me constant, welcome company, and
will be faithful to the end; so, until we meet again, be it
in this world or beyond the Golden Gate, Old Friends . . .
So-long!